THE VETERAN
ADVANTAGE

THE VETERAN ADVANTAGE

The Battlefield to Entrepreneurship

TYLER REISER

NEW DEGREE PRESS

THE VETERAN ADVANTAGE

The Battlefield to Entrepreneurship

ISBN   978-1-64137-364-7 *Paperback*

        978-1-64137-708-9   *Ebook*

Contents

This book is dedicated to our brothers and sisters who didn't make it home.

The Veteran Advantage

"And the reality is you can generalize everyone; the military is a microcosm of America. So you get a slice of everything."
—DONNY O'MALLEY (INTERVIEW)

Reaction Under Fire:

Seven, eight, nine, ten. Casey finishes his round of dips. Looking around at the gym, with its clamshell shape and a snap together floor with weights and rusty cardio equipment filling up the space, he hears sound reminiscent of training. "Somebody's getting some," he thinks to himself as he hears the crackling of gunshots in the distance. It's his third day in Afghanistan, at a small base that according to Casey is "the size of a Walmart parking lot."

"We start seeing the impacts on the ground and we realize, 'Oh, they're firing at us!'" As they run to the wall to return fire, there was screech of an RPG followed by an explosion, hitting a barrier next to the gym Casey had just come from. "I didn't even have my body armor on...I just went straight to the wall. Everyone was going to the wall." With the base under attack, he thinks, "Welcome to Afghanistan. This just got real. I saw a tower and went up into it and started returning fire." He looks through his optic and notices two motorcycle riders driving back and forth shooting at the base and others popping up here and there shooting rockets and automatic rifles.

Casey takes aim and fires a burst, hitting in front of the motorcycle. "So then I just readjusted, and I shot two more, just two more rounds, and then a big cloud of tan dust erupted—*it didn't even feel real, kind of like a video game*—and the firefight continued."

"We weren't even out on a mission yet." Casey recalled the early days of his active deployment. Sometimes an everyday act like going to the gym can evolve into a life-or-death decision at a moment's notice. Nobody wants to be in this position, but it's required on the battlefield to ensure safety for yourself and others around you. You must remain vigilant at every moment, even at "home."

* * *

Years later, Casey's skills learned in the military—*leadership, brotherhood, resilience, and mental toughness*—have enabled him to grow a successful franchise in Texas where he continues to learn while expanding his abilities as an entrepreneur.

It wasn't always this way. Like many other veterans, he struggles to find purpose during transition, isolating himself, not communicating with other veterans, and ultimately thinking he can face the world alone.

He stumbles deeper down a dark alley of life, leading to his arrest. Feeling lost—guilt, depression, as well as rage consumed him at his low.

Taking ownership of his story, he takes advantage of his second chance, transforming himself and finding purpose in entrepreneurship.

* * *

Every year, approximately 200,000 military members transition into civilian life, according to the Henry M. Jackson Foundation for the Advancement of Military Medicine.[1] Additionally, there will be approximately 3.4 million post-9/11 veterans by 2020, many of whom have experienced combat and the battlefield.[2]

Transitioning out of the military often includes a series of adjustments, such as new geographic location, career, relationships, family roles, support systems, social networks, and community.[3] These challenges lead to diverse outcomes, and the first try at transition doesn't always go as planned.

Waking Up

Hopefully it doesn't take a dramatic event, like Casey's run in with the law, to wake us up and start listening to our individual needs. Fortunately for him, he was given a second chance.

I personally know second chances well. As a former bomb technician, I feel like my life has been one long series of second chances. Training for anything, we

---

1   (The Veterans Metrics Initiative. 2018)
2   (Department of Veterans Affairs, 2015)
3   (Castro, Kintzle, & Hassan, 2014)

have to prepare for everything. During my time, our training began in Texas. First, a two-week preliminary course, just after basic training. After weeding out half our class, our instructors shipped us off to Florida for nine months of intensive training at the Naval School of Explosive Ordnance Disposal. The instructors forced us to learn fast, adapt, or fail. With the motto "Initial Success or Total Failure," the school doesn't think too highly of failure. Having successfully sprinted through a minefield of intense training, it was time to go to our first unit.

Learning the tools and techniques available to operate in any environment took time, but we trained often. Honing our skills quickly took deliberate practice and instruction from people with more experience. Learning quickly was the only way to stay adaptable to the ever-changing battle space.

I arrived at my first unit in mid-2004. The War in Afghanistan had been going on for a few years, and the Iraq War was just beginning to kick off. I was nineteen. Improvised explosive devices (IEDs) weren't even a mainstream idea yet. *The Hurt Locker* would have been sci-fi, not Hollywood artistry. By 2008, the landscape had changed dramatically.

I can easily remember the first time I saw an IED unexpectedly go off. It was the scariest thing I'd ever seen, and also the day I decided to live my life to the fullest.

One day, we are driving down the road and BOOM—the vehicle in front of us vanishes into thin air. Five brothers lost. Nothing left but a hole in the ground.

"Where is the secondary?" we think as we try to move our vehicle out of the kill zone.

It is time to get to work. We're on a mission, and there is no time to think about what just happened, come up with a plan, and act. As a member of an EOD team, we had a mission, and we were trained for it.

Protect people, protect property, remove the threat: our mission never changes no matter which mission we're on. We conduct various missions—they are usually boring, always life threatening, and our orders come in from higher (command).

"We need you to clear the route, disarm that bomb, or see if that "suspicious" thing is a piece of trash or an IED." Some missions were planned, and some were in real time. It was impossible to know when the next would occur. At the completion of every mission, we had a second chance to reset our gear, analyze our resources, and train on a tool or technique that was needing practice to be better the next time we went out.

When a mission ends, there is time to reflect. The luck I had walking away unharmed, when only moments in time made a difference, forced me to wake up. It changed my perspective on life: I decided to enjoy the gift we have, follow my passion, and persevere through the challenges life presents me.

Transition

I took the easy route. My expertise in IEDs was in demand, and the defense industry dangles a decent paycheck in front of a transitioning service member. Continuing my career in defense would lead me to another two years in Afghanistan in various positions, fighting the proliferation of IEDs.

Growing weary of the long hours and harsh living conditions of deployments, it became clear I would not remain in defense forever. I put my head down, saving almost every penny of my earnings for two years. I was prepared to begin my transition to a new career, but first, it was time for some much-needed R&R.

On May 5, 2013, I quit my job and flew from Afghanistan to Thailand to pursue my passion for scuba diving. It was a trip that would take me literally around the world and offer an entirely new perspective on life—one without so much violence.

In my travels, I explored many nations, cultures, and undersea creatures. Along the way, and with many others, I broke a world record, circumnavigated the globe, and had the time of my life.

After seven years overseas, it was time to come back to the United States to start a new career, eventually leading to entrepreneurship. The road has been full of challenges, requiring additional skills and knowledge to attempt to survive in today's fast paced world.

This book is meant to save the reader time looking for entrepreneurial resources in an information-dense environment. After writing and deleting and researching and writing and interviewing and deleting, I hope to provide a starting point for your research.

The Veteran Advantage demonstrates that skill and passion come from years of experience and difficult times. Through our demanding actions, we grow until we are capable of things we could never have imagined.

In Part One, I give insights into the focused actions and resilience during moments of chaos on the battlefield, a superpower often forgotten after transition that when harnessed again leads to a transformative life.

Part Two looks inward to identify purpose, develop a plan, and test ideas before diving in headfirst. It is about learning to find passion and being the best we can be everyday as we pursue what is important to us, starting to plan quickly and adapting to the world around us—finding and following success.

As an idea gains traction, the entrepreneur will need a vast support system to stand any chance of success. Part Three discusses the importance of building and engaging a network, identifying the proper forms of capital, and building a company through leadership and culture.

Part Four is one of the shortest but also one of the most important pieces of this book. When the fear feels too great, or the burden seems too much, like the warrior on the chaotic battlefield you must act— facing the enemy and returning fire.

Entrepreneurship

I am not an expert in entrepreneurship.

Sure, I've built a couple hobby business—selling gum balls to my classmates in first grade, trying to develop land while in the military, leasing rental property, renting specialized dive equipment, importing beach chairs. I was always driven to work on something, sometimes succeeding, sometimes failing, and always learning. Pursuing something more than a hobby required me to go through a more challenging transformation than any other in my life, and it took expertise I did not have.

Over the last year, I've been interviewing successful veteran entrepreneurs like Mark Rockefeller, Taylor Justice, Doug Doan, and many more to gather their lessons learned. Combining these interviews with further research provides a framework for the process of being an entrepreneur in the new economy. While their stories have some common themes, they are also very different, and there's a lot of wisdom to be shared.

You'll hear stories and insights including:

- Several transitions out of the military taking various turns that are described by veteran entrepreneur Jeremy Green as "a perpetual stumbling of sorts." Taking lessons from each correction, they find themselves combining their skills of the past into an effective business. Jeremy's story leads him from side hustles in Panama and Korea to owning several businesses in the Philippines with his wife and newborn.

- Donny O'Malley manages the chaos of a veteran media machine, capable of producing a $100,000 budget production with his friends and family every six weeks. His detailed planning methods with roots in the Marine Corps planning process enables him to pull off what "has never been done by anyone in Hollywood."
- Ideas and concepts from prominent thought leaders on the topics of finite vs. infinite games, tapping into passion and perseverance, and how veteran business owners like William Treseder use a daily practice of purpose to ensure he is always improving what is most important.
- You will face challenges as you begin to test your ideas and find the products and services ready for market. In the beginning, they are only hypothesis. Through agile and lean methods, entrepreneurs like Sam Meek build, test, and possibly discard products in a matter of weeks, finding the right product market fit.

By the end of this book, you will see that life and entrepreneurship are just a series of second chances, some starting off quiet and uneventful and others starting with an awakening, like Casey Lawrence firefight while lifting weights in Afghanistan. No matter how it begins, you'll find life leading you down a seemingly wandering path, each experience building upon the last until you are ready to achieve more than you could ever imagine.

This book is for the combat veteran with the entrepreneurial spirit who wants to transition their skills into business. With time, experience, and support, you will develop

The Veteran Advantage

How To Use This Book

Depending on who you are, you may read this book a little differently. There may a chapter or two you feel you really have questions about—feel free to jump ahead. You may miss an introduction to one of the veteran entrepreneurs interviewed in the book, but you can catch up on that later. If instead you'd like to read it cover to cover and come back to complete the exercises, that's fine too.

What's most important is to understand that we are always in transition and growing all the time—all of us. If we are action oriented, we can overcome any obstacles that may get in our way. This book shows some barriers others who came before us have faced and tips to get around, over, under, or through them. Choose a topic you're struggling with, and start there. Reach out to the people interviewed in this book and others asking for support. Some may help.

If you are reading this book and provide support to veterans or entrepreneurs, identify opportunities to assist others in these challenging topics. Share your wisdom and expertise; they take a lot of mistakes to learn. Support others as others have supported you on your journey.

Finally, if you're in the trenches as an entrepreneur, understand you're not alone. These challenges are faced by many and better faced together. Find your tribe, work together, keep learning, and leverage each other's skills. These topics can be a starting point for discussion, research, and action. Use them to learn more and grow faster by adapting your knowledge and testing your ideas. "We need you to change the world." –Mark Rockefeller

Part 1

Combat and Transition

Chapter 1

Focus Amid Chaos

"We introduce our students, almost from day one, to absolute chaos, and they will struggle." –Robert Herbert

Leadership in the military forces you to overcome and find a way to solve the problem. Not always having the right tools, we must be adaptable, do more with less, and make it happen either way. Building a business is no different. Remember the skills from your experience and how they apply today.

Preparation

"Reiser, you've got orders to Afghanistan. You begin your training cycle next month," says my commander at our morning meeting. "Hell yeah," I think to myself as I look at the list of pre-deployment training. A shooting school in South Carolina, combat training with the Army, Explosive Ordnance Disposal (EOD) specific training—the list goes on. Over the next month, we prepare our gear and train with our unit.

Our brothers and sisters in our unit review the current threats in our theater of war and begin designing scenarios for us to solve. They ask us if we're ready to go, and we agree. Somewhere out in the woods, they have constructed some of the most challenging real-world scenarios ever faced by individuals in our field. They tell us the "standard nonsense" that provides almost no real details of what we're dealing with. "We saw some suspicious stuff about 200 meters down that way, past the curve and by a rock." Time to get to work.

Coming together, we come up with a plan. When life and death are at stake, everyone has a say, but this is no democracy. Equipped with robots, explosives, and bomb suits, we start setting up. The tasks are set, and we begin.

"Hey, asshole, you find anything yet?" yells the team lead as he's making sure he's all prepped. "No, where the hell did he say it was?" I respond while staring diligently at the robot control screen showing an eight-inch display of the bouncing ground in front of my robot. "He said it's by a rock after the curve on the left, about two hundred meters down," says the team lead. "Great directions, after the rock? I must have passed it, I'll come back." Looking at the time, the team lead continues, "Forty-five minutes on scene—let's hurry up!"

"I've been back and forth four times now and haven't seen anything! Do we know anything else?" I ask, frustrated with trying to find this "rock." "We've been here too long; I'm suiting up and going down," the team lead replies. Knowing the risk he'll be taking, we question the decision. "Wait, give me another ten minutes," I say, but he insists. "OK, let's get you suited up."

"You're all set. You know your plan? What is it?" I ask, doing one final check with my team lead to make sure he's thinking clearly. "See you when you get back," I say to him as I lowered his one-inch, bulletproof glass face shield. He begins his two hundred-meter walk down the trail, enclosed in a eighty-plus-pound suit, into the unknown. Looking for anything out of place and remembering the plan, he continues down the path.

"OK, about two hundred meters, I must be at about fifty now," he thinks to himself while looking all around. "One hundred meters, halfway there." He is beginning to get winded from the heavy suit. "One hundred fifty meters. It could be anywhere now; what did he say again? Was it fifty meters after the rock? Or the curve?"

He can't quite remember the conversation more than an hour ago. It's hard to breath with all this gear on, and hard to think as well. "I should be close," he reassures himself as he looks everywhere for any signs.

All of a sudden, in the distance, we hear a loud BOOM. The team leader is dead. Nearby, a squealing buzzer continues sounding as we all realized what had happened. "Damn," we all think as we regroup. "Too much went wrong." "We're too slow." "I can't believe I couldn't find it and made you go down range." We start putting it all on the table, realizing how bad we suck and how much work we have left to get ready.

Fortunately, this situation was only training, with simulation explosives and loud buzzers. If we operated like this in a war zone, lives would be at risk. "This is why we're doing this—you guys gotta get better," says another tech who has just returned from the battlefield and is now facilitating our training. We would spend the next several months doing just that. From tactical driving and evasion to cultural sensitivity, the training was diverse and intense for a young twenty-three-year-old preparing for a second round of battle.

Our training was useful.

* * *

Being well trained for a complex dynamic tasks like clearing a battlefield of IEDs is paramount, and we are only one cog in this massive machine. Each and every specialty must know their role inside and out. They must then work together to achieve their mission, both individually and on teams large and small.

An article by the Army in 2006 describing our EOD-specific training states, "The insurgents have made the improvised explosive device one of their main weapons against coalition forces. The purpose of this course is to ensure Explosive Ordnance Disposal personnel know the intelligence, tools and procedures, needed when dealing with these devices."[4] We attend our set of training, everyone else is preparing in other ways.

For the 26th Marine Infantry, over the six-month spin-up training the participants "progress through curriculum and exercises that teach individual, small unit, and unit tactics while integrating the separate elements into a cohesive, flexible and powerful force."[5]

---

4   (US Army, 2006)

5   (26thmeu.marines.mil, 2019)

Their training will include "Amphibious Operations, Mechanized and Helicopter-borne Raids, Noncombatant Evacuation Operations, Humanitarian Assistance, and Urban Operations."[6] They train at every level from the individual to the entire force, and this experience is the true power.

On the battlefield, things change rapidly. The military trains for success by ensuring that everyone knows their part, knows what decisions they can and can't make, and recognizes their mission within the broader context. Each part is an individual, autonomous entity while also being a part of multiple autonomous teams, each with its own limits. Every person is part leader, follower, and peer, all at the same time. These roles become more apparent the further you move up the Special Teams ladder.

* * *

One of the more elite military teams, the Navy SEALs, live and train together so much that they can operate almost as a single entity.

---

6   (26thmeu.marines.mil, 2019)

"We introduce our students, almost from day-one, to absolute chaos and they will struggle," says Robert Herbert, a Navy SEAL commanding officer.[7]

"When you look at historic mistakes on the battlefield, they're almost always associated with fear or panic, so the capacity to control these impulses is extremely important."[8] From the start, their training is so intense that out of 140 candidates, only an average thirty-six SEALS-in-training will graduate.

"They're trying to introduce you to the fact that panic is going to be less and less an option throughout your career," says Chuck Pfarrer, a former Navy SEAL. David Eagleman says, "The right way to do training is to expose people to scary situations where they can get used to them and know how to react when they're confronted with the real thing."[9]

Desensitized from the battlefield after months of training in conditions that are as close to reality as possible, our journey begins. The training could never prepare us for it, but it would hopefully save our lives.

---

7   (The Brain, 2008)

8   (The Brain, 2008)

9   (The Brain, 2008)

Decades At war

"As of December 2011, roughly 74 percent of AC (active component) soldiers had deployed to Iraq and/or Afghanistan," according to a RAND study. Most of the remainder are in training or not available.[10]

There have been millions of "troop-years" of total time in these wars.[11] Let me repeat that: MILLIONS of troop YEARS...and these are not safe places.

"All told, between 480,000 and 507,000 people have been killed in the United States' post-9/11 wars in Iraq, Afghanistan, and Pakistan." According to Neta C. Crawford at the Watson Institute for International and Public Affairs at Brown University.[12]

As a former bomb tech in the US Department of Defense between 2003 and 2009 and intelligence support until 2013, I know the effects of this fight all too well.

Multiple countries riddled with hazardous devices where your first step could be your last: anything you touch, anything you move, everywhere, everything, and everyone. In spite of the risk, we task these young men

---

10   (The RAND Corporation, 2013)
11   (The RAND Corporation, 2013)
12   (Crawford, 2018)

and women with going out in the field and completing their missions.

Whether a cook or a member of the Special Forces, anytime you could be told to get your gear and step outside the wire. You were trained for this, and it's time to put that training to use; your life and the lives of those next to you depend on it.

You're never fully ready.

Deployment

For Justin Rettenberger, the mission was to train the Afghan military, get them out in the fight, and take back control of an area. He recounts the story on Donny O'Malley's "Irreverent Warriors" series.

Coordinating with the local Afghan General caused the initial challenges. Only five or six soldiers show up after the General had promised a thousand. Using the promises of military equipment, the general was convinced to corral 500 troops. Rettenberger and the team fit the Afghans with all the gear they need for the upcoming mission.

4:00 a.m., thirty minutes past mission kickoff, the Afghans finally begin to arrive. "This rag-tag group looks nothing

*like those we equipped. What happened to your equipment?"
Rettenberger asks one of the soldiers. "I needed money and
sold it," the Afghan soldier replied. "Great, at least about two
hundred of you showed up!" Rettenberger says to himself. It's
time to start the mission.*

*Two days into the journey across the desert while linking
up with another unit to get communications back up, their
vehicle strikes a 120-pound IED, blowing off the entire front
quarter of their vehicle. Bleeding, confused, and in need of
medical assistance, they regain their senses and find their
only option for evacuation is to continue by ground.*

*They move on and things only get worse. Bullets start flying
as a firefight develops all around. Justin instinctively leaps
out of the vehicle, laying down on the ground, and returns
fire at the enemy.*

*His fire draws the enemy to his location, and rounds start
coming at him. A few more rounds down range, he finally
hits the enemy.*

*All of a sudden, his hearing returns. "Get back in the truck!!"
he hears his team yelling. He realizes he's out in the open with
no cover for protection. A teammate runs out and grabs him.
"Staff sergeant, you need to get back in the truck!" he yells.
"OK," Justin replies.*

"You just shot that guy!" his driver yell as he gets back in the truck. "Could I have a cigarette?" Justin replies. "I don't even smoke, it seemed like the thing to do....That was wild."

Machine guns firing on both sides, the convoy continues forward onto the "hardball"—a paved road. The machine gun fire starts to dissipate toward the back of the convoy and then stops completely as the convoy gets closer to the base.

This part of their journey ends—having delivered the Afghan soldiers closer, this mission was over. Most would be off on their next mission soon. Injured from being blown up by an IED, he needed to get medical attention and head home.[13]

* * *

Seven, eight, nine, ten. Casey finishes his round of dips in the gym. Looking around at the gym, with its clamshell shape and a snap together floor with weights and rusty cardio equipment filling up the space, he hears sound reminiscent of training. "Somebody's getting some," he thinks to himself as he hears the crackling of gunshots in the distance. It's his third day in Afghanistan, at a small base that according to Casey is "the size of a Walmart parking lot."

---

13   *(YouTube, 2015)*

"We start seeing the impacts on the ground and we realize, 'Oh, they're firing at US!'" As they run to the wall to return fire, there was screech of an RPG followed by an explosion, hitting a barrier next to the gym Casey had just came from.

"I didn't even have my body armor on...I just went straight to the wall. Everyone was going to the wall."

With the base under attack he thought, "Welcome to Afghanistan. This just got real. I saw a tower and went up into it and started returning fire." He looked through his optic and noticed two motorcycle riders driving back and forth shooting at the base, and others popping up here and there shooting rockets and automatic rifles.

Casey takes aim and fires a burst, hitting in front of the motorcycle. "So then I just readjusted, and I shot two more, just two more rounds, and then a big huge cloud of tan dust erupted. The firefight continued."

"We weren't even out on a mission yet."

In a war zone, sometimes you're not on a mission, and an everyday act like going to the gym can evolve into a life-or-death decision at a moments notice. Nobody wants to be in this position, but it's required on the battlefield to ensure safety for yourself and others around you. You must remain vigilant at every moment, even at "home."

Summary

The battlefield is incredibly complex and uncertain. These stories touch on the preparation and dedication those in combat must exhibit. These individuals were told to go to implement their training in some of the most hostile locations on Earth, sometimes for more than a year at a time.

In modern battle, like entrepreneurship, every step is potentially your last, but with every step comes knowledge and experience. The mental fortitude and skills developed during these times should not be forgotten; they should be developed and applied.

This kind of situation is what we are trained for: to survive, adapt, and even excel in such environments. While nothing can prepare a human for war, when we've identified a mission, we go do it. Coordinating with local tribal elders, building schools, providing medical care to the locals, getting shot at, and dodging explosive devices are all part of the package.

Moving forward on the journey, we'll discover new challenges that require as much preparation, passion, and perseverance as the harshest moments of battle. Keeping a warrior mindset will help you on the journey.

In this chapter, we've examined how individuals like Casey were able to keep their heads using quick thinking, unparalleled focus, and stress management tactics. These skills were paramount to his survival out on the battlefield, and now they're some of the most valuable skills he'll use when he enters into a new kind of battlefield: the private sector.

In his entrepreneurial journey, Casey will have to demonstrate extreme focus over extended periods of time as he develops his business model, quick thinking when he negotiates sales with customers, and stress management tactics when he is inevitably faced with adversity.

* * *

- Modern combat is an intense environment in which any step could be your last.
- Most post–9/11 service members deploy to combat zones.

- To survive combat, it takes focus, quick thinking and stress management.
- Identify two skills you will train with as much intensity as the military.
- Write down a time when life was chaotic and you were able to keep your cool.

Chapter 2

Everyone Transitions

"Whether you're Chairman of the Joint Chiefs of Staff Dempsey, after 43 years, or you're a lieutenant, or a young captain who's got out after six years, or whatever the hell you served, everybody transitions." –Doug Doan

* * *

"There are at least two kinds of games. One could be called finite, the other infinite. A finite game is played for the purpose of winning, an infinite game for the purpose of continuing the play," says James Carse in his book titled *Finite and Infinite Games*.[14]

Finite games are quite familiar, as we play them from a very young age. T-ball, checkers, and tic-tac-toe are all finite games. The rules are known, the players agree

---

14   (Carse, 2013)

to play, and there is a definitive start and end. Infinite games are not so intuitive.

"In an infinite game, there are known and unknown players, the rules are changeable, and the objective is to perpetuate the game or stay in the game as long as possible," says Simon Sinek during a talk at The New York Times Conference. The point is not to win—it's to keep playing.[15]

"In a finite game, the rules are fixed until there is a winner, but in an infinite game, the rules must change during the course of play.", says Sinek. The rules continue to change which creates a constant challenge but it also creates a world of opportunity for those who can adapt. While you continue to play the ever-changing infinite game you will find the game is only played against yourself and your goal is to continue and improve.[16]

An infinite game may take the form of the Marines on a mission to deliver the Afghan troops, perpetuating the survival of themselves and those around them, hopefully long enough to come back safe, or of William, as you'll see later, in an infinite game of education following his own rules to advance from a failed student to

15   (Sinek, 2019)
16   (Sinek, 2019)

Stanford University graduate by incrementally getting better through self-improvement. Each step in the journey through the infinite game prepares us for the next. Adapting, improving, and perpetuating the game will all be important.

Transition

We all go through transitions in the infinite game of life. Some are easier than others, but it's always challenging when it's you who's in it. For the military member, you will have the choice or eventually be forced to make a major transition, one that will uproot your life, reset your network, and force you to learn a new craft. You will make it out the other side; however, the growth required will be painful.

Remember your training and experience. See you on the other side...

Getting Lucky

"Maybe I would like real estate? What's required of that? Do I need a license? I could go to school at the U of M to get a degree, that could work," I think to myself as I research possible school and job combinations for the future. Twenty-two-year-old me had no idea what

I really wanted in life and only a few months to figure it out.

The first three months of the deployment were at Forward Operating Base Asadabad a small base in northeast Afghanistan, home to the infamous Korengal Valley, later named "The Valley of Death." Clearing routes of IEDs and getting in firefights were a normal occurrence. Being stuck on main base was a different experience.

I am three months away from returning from my second deployment and three months and one week away from separation from the military after my six-year commitment. The anticipation is killing me. I keep checking emails, browsing the internet, and praying for a mission. The impending countdown and the lack of operations cause time to nearly stop.

Out of the blue, Troy, the civilian lab manager of a supporting forensics group, asks our unit for assistance. "We're way behind and could use your help; we have a one thousand-case backlog!" the lab manager says to a group of twenty or so bomb techs, "We'll teach you everything," he continues. My curiosity is piqued.

"So, you're going to teach us forensics and we'll work in the lab with you when were not on mission?" I ask the lab manager thinking about an escape. "You've got it., Troy replies in his good-natured tone.

"I'm in," I say as the first volunteer, thinking this task would surely cure my boredom.

Super glue chambers, ultraviolet light, fingerprints, and DNA are all topics of discussion over the next few months. As a science lover, it's great. Troy and the others are fantastic teachers, and they let us dive right in.

Within no time, we are developing fingerprints and sending DNA samples across to our sister lab for processing. The next couple of months rush by while we learn how to apply forensic science to the counter-improvised explosive device fight.

Near my time to depart, the lab manager asks me,

"What's next?".

Having no idea, I say, "I'll probably go back home and go to school." Shaking his head, Troy says, "Come work for us."

A few weeks later, I embark on the second half of my defense career. A fortuitous moment leading to a career opportunity, I imagine how amazing civilian life would be, not realizing how narrowly I escaped an unplanned transition.

Try and Try Again

Sam Meek's transition started off quite normal, moving back home after the military. After getting a job as a caddie, one fateful day, his supervisor introduces him to a member about to start golfing for the day. "Sam, come over here and meet Walter McKay; you'll be caddying for him today."

At the end of the day on the course, Walter asks, "Do you know anything about the hedge funds, Sam?"

"Nothing." Sam replies.

"Great, I'd like to invite you to my office to give you a tour," Walter continueds as he writes down the address. "Come by tomorrow."

"See you tomorrow," Sam responds, reaching out to collect the address.

Sam doesn't know what to think of it—what was the purpose for the tour? There was no way this is for a job;

he had no experience, and they didn't even talk about it. No matter the purpose, Sam had a problem: he knows he needs a suit.

Browsing the aisles of Goodwill, he finds the suit section and starts his search. After looking through everything, the best he can find was a suit about one size too big. It will have to do.

Nervous and confused, Sam arrives to meet Walter. Moments later, Walter begins walking him around the office in a round-robin fashion and introduces him to the eleven employees in the office.

"Is this some kind of incognito interview?" Sam wonders to himself as he meets the next person. Walter takes his time ensuring everyone has a chance to meet Sam. The tour was over.

A bit disappointed at not having the opportunity to be interviewed, Sam thanks Walter for the tour and turns to leave when Walter asks a final question.

"What do you think, Sam—are you ready to start Monday?"

"I was Walt's personal CRM [Client Relationship Management tool]; he would take phone calls and I would take notes." Sam recalled the early days of working for Walter. It wasn't long before he had picked up on Walt's sales process and how he was building relationships. Soon, he would be sent off on his own.

Sam starts immediately, applying all the techniques he had learned from Walter through their time working together, and it worked. He starts making sale after sale, applying the craft Walter taught him. Business was booming.

Everything was going great, until the United States went through a massive credit crunch, the likes of which had never been seen. It was the crash of 2009—The Great Recession. Now, a company with sixty employees, managing over a BILLION dollars of assets, had to bow to the powers of the market.

Sam was the second-to-last person out the door on the final day of the hedge fund. He helped Walter until the end and was now in transition once again.

* * *

"This is the end. The next bullet is for me. The world's over. Soon, I will be in peace. How did I end up here? What led me to this point?" Casey thinks to himself.

After the infantry, his transition led him to the oil fields of Texas, where he had been living in an RV while working. The lack of mission or passion led him down a path of depression with seemingly no way out. Then he was fired.

His girlfriend just left him, and it had been a hard day. Getting drunk to deal with the recent events only escalated the problem. Things got way out of control.

"I had a standoff with the SWAT team and sheriff's department down on the border," Casey told me in an interview.

"I wanted them to do it."

Surrounding him, the SWAT team begins to move in to take him down, and, with no reason left to live, he waits for his end. Little did he know, his journey was only beginning.

"I'm a big guy—they never roughed me up, they didn't tase me, just arrested me and took me to jail."

Surprised by the outcome, he snaps back into reality and is forced to examine his life. Thinking back to that day Casey, recalled the feeling he had when he was released. He had an opportunity and a duty to do more. He thought,

"I have a fresh start again."

Second Chances

"I dropped out the first time I went to community college, after high school. I enrolled and then I flunked out, within a couple months."

William Treseder's early academic career was not the model outcome. "I had terrible, terrible grades in high school. I graduated in the fifth percentile of my class," William said. It didn't get much better after high school, so he decided to move on.

He was now getting in shape to join the Marine Corps. He wouldn't think about school again until he transitioned.

It was 2005, and he had just completed his military duty in the Marine Corps with a specialty in combat arms. With no plan in place, "I just did what I think a lot of people do, which I usually don't recommend people do, but I just went home." Coming from California, he decided to move back to his hometown. "First I lived with my parents for a couple months and then with my grandmother."

William decided to give community college a second chance, now with the experience of a Marine.

"Even though I didn't really know what I was doing at first, I was just able to brute force everything," William told me. His professors would have open office hours for students to come ask questions, so he went to every single one. "I was too naive to know that you shouldn't do that." His new approach was working.

Starting from the most basic point of not failing, he put a telltale military approach of crawl, walk, and run into effect.

"First, it was like, don't get an F."

"You know, just like don't trip over your own feet when you're trying to march, right? Or, learning the basics of marksmanship, or the basics of whatever.

"First, it was don't get an F, then shoot for a B, then shoot for an A, and, finally, only get As. By the time you get to that point, this is the routine, this is how I do this; if I follow these rules, I work this hard, and this is going to be the result." He had trained himself to succeed in academia, and he was just beginning.

"I took the first class every day, I took classes all the way until the afternoon, then I did some student government stuff or other things in the community, then drove home, did homework and went to bed."

Repurposing his Marine strengths, his next acceptance letter was into Stanford.

Perpetual Stumbling

Once you get out, there is no basic training for civilian life. "I was just in a perpetual stumbling of sorts, like an Airborne shuffle, when you get to the twelfth or fourteenth kilometer and your feet start to give," Jeremie Green said, comparing long ruck marches to making the transition into entrepreneurship. "If I do nothing, then I'm going to end up on the street, but hey, maybe if I put pen to paper and come up with something, maybe I can trade ideas for millions instead of hours for dollars."

Pushing his way forward after transition led him on his journey to do just that.

Summary

Life is an infinite game that involves many transitions and transformations. As a military member or veteran, you will be forced to experience the abrupt life changes of separation. The stumbling nature of your exploration to find your next mission will be challenging and require perseverance, patience, and an inward look at your skills and experience of past times to account for what's made you who you are today. Keep moving, and you'll make it out the other side.

* * *

- Everyone transitions; it is a part of life.
- Transition is a form of perpetual stumbling, and it takes time to find the right path. Don't beat yourself up if it doesn't go right at first.
- There are infinite games and finite games: life and business are infinite games. The only objective is to compete against yourself to improve.
- Think about your past experiences and what skill sets you have developed over time. Write down at least five.

- Recall three experiences that were challenging but, through perseverance, you overcame.
- Speak with five people who know you well and ask them what your strengths are.

Part 2

Redefining Your Mission

Shifting your mind-set from the battlefield to business will be key in your success. Don't lose the lessons learned—adapt them to the new environment. Learn new skills that apply to business and merge them with your current understanding about operating in complex uncertain environments.

Part two discusses lean methodologies that apply experimentation to business. Taking from science and manufacturing practices, as well as a more recent adoption of lean principles in the tech space, no longer should we follow an arduous process to release products and services but, instead, rapidly iterate to find the right answer.

By the end of Part Two, you'll have a starting place to research technology and techniques, enabling you to fail quickly and cheaply to succeed faster. You'll learn frameworks to business models and techniques to find the right product to bring to market. You'll also learn how the skills you already know from mission planning will give you the skills to develop your own missions to build and test the models you hypothesize.

These interviews and the research involved have changed my thinking about how to build a business. They have also given me permission to test ideas without fear of failure. It is my hope that this book does the same for you.

Chapter 3

Mission

"Purpose is a frequently misunderstood concept: It isn't a thing that can be found, it isn't stable over time, and it isn't a single, solitary thing. Instead, purpose is something that you must build. It comes from focusing on the meaningful parts of your work and striving to instill everything you do with purpose. Look for multiple source of meaning that can help you find value in your work and life, and recognize that your purpose is not a stagnant concept; it will change as your roles, commitments, and personal endeavors evolve."
–John Coleman

Mission or Depression

"I'm fighting a mission I believe in: it's a mission of virtue, it's the best I've ever felt since the United States Marine Corps," says Rudy Reyes, co-founder of Force Blue. He didn't always feel that way; at his low, he nearly committed suicide. (Reyes, 2019) This dichotomy of light and darkness showcases the reality every human faces as they find a life full of meaning or one of darkness and depression.

Rudy, a former Recon Marine, was a trained combat diver but never had the chance to see the true beauty of the ocean until he took a dive trip with Jim Ritterhoff. Jim thought Rudy was in a dark spot when he suggested the trip. Rudy reluctantly agreed to a moment that would pull him out of depression and back into a mission mind-set.

Seeing the densely packed diverse life on the coral reefs for the first time is mind-boggling. There are so many species roaming around looking for food, next to strange creatures you could never have imagined. The reef is an ecosystem coming to life all around you. As a combat diver, Rudy would have been fortunate if he could see his hands through the murky, night-filled waters he was likely to find himself in. The reef during daylight is something else completely: Rudy was changed.

Not long after, he was talking about his experience with other divers when he learned about the massive destruction of coral reefs around the world. Rudy was called to action to make a difference. "What more honorable thing is there to do, than to help the things in crisis, and that needs your love, attention and strength."[17]

Rudy and his team support the reefs and the oceans in Florida and beyond. His ability to work on something "bigger than yourself" has created something in him and others that has been lost since the military: a mission.[18]

"I couldn't have started Force Blue unless I had been through all the highs and lows, the abandonment, the anger and the shame, to do a course correction and rallying myself back up and think about what really is important," says Reyes.[19]

Sharing Force Blue's mission with other combat divers has led to the term "Mission Therapy"—assisting others in realizing a sense of purpose. "Getting back into service and living for something that is pure—it's been paramount to my success now," says Rudy. According to him, to achieve that success requires four pillars: physical fitness, community and brotherhood, mother nature, and a mission. "You need all four in balance; with that you can do anything."[20]

---

17   (Reyes and Ritterhoff, 2017)
18   (Reyes and Ritterhoff, 2017)
19   (Reyes, 2019)
20   (Reyes, 2019)

*　*　*

How do combat veterans successfully navigate the battlefield amid firefights and bomb explosions, yet often struggle transitioning into the civilian sector? One of the initial problems is that we're used to missions. When we know our mission, our mind-set and training kick in, and there is no stopping us.

When we get out, nobody is telling the problem that needs to be solved, leaving us mission-less. The "higher" authority has vanished, leaving us, possibly for the first time in our adult lives, with our own choices.

"Without a defined sense of purpose, men can begin to wander. They become less motivated to stay active and engaged, and it eventually can trickle down and weaken both their physical and mental health," says Fred Silverstone, a licensed mental health counselor.[21] Identifying direction after the military is no easy task.

"It's normal to feel anger, loss, anxiety, or fear about having to adjust to changes in one's life," says Silverstone.[22] It's OK to have these thoughts, but it's a lot like the morale of troops: negativity leads to negativity

---

21　(Silverstone, 2018)

22　(Silverstone, 2018)

and positivity leads to positivity. Silverstone suggests replacing negative self-talk with positive. Think of the challenges you have faced to this point and think to yourself, "If I can do all of that, I'll get through this."

Keeping a positive morale won't be enough, becoming your own "higher" involves identifying something that needs to be achieved that is interesting and meaningful to you. It has nothing to do with what you used to do; it's about you, today. We must create our own mission. It begins with reverse planning: we must start with where we're trying to go.

Find a Mission

Why do we need a mission? When troops are on the battlefield, the mission drives everything. Soldiers need to know what needs to be accomplished, who's involved, and what support is available. This deep understanding of the battle space enables complex shifts in multiteam strategy during a chaotic event like a firefight. The mission exists to guide all individual and group actions and actors.

"The higher the goal, the more it is an end in and of itself," says Angela Duckworth, author of *Grit: The Power of Passion and Perseverance.* Like a compass heading, the direction remains constant as you navigate the path. These are infrequently changed and not actually achievable when they are developed thoughtfully. They are guides from which to make all other decisions.[23]

Will you find this overnight? No. It will start from within, taking account of who you are as a person and finding something to work on that seems close. Through trial and error, a mission will become more clear as you gain experience. Pivoting many times will lead you closer as you achieve smaller tasks that support your mission, simplifying these tasks over time into a guiding force.

A bomb tech's highest-level goals are preserving life, property, and equipment; all other goals work to achieve those ends. Within this concept, we can filter each of the decisions we were making through the hierarchy. For instance, would you risk your life to save a piece of equipment? What about a piece of equipment to save somebody's house?

The choices are easy to make when the highest-level goals are well-defined. If the task adds to the highest-level goal, it should be included; if not, it should be

---

23 (Duckworth, 2016)

reconsidered. The challenge early on, if you don't have any experience, is choosing a direction and pivoting early and often.

Starting a business or challenging endeavor is no different; the pain and suffering you will go through will be intense. The winding trail it will take to find its fit will take a lot of time and energy. Having a mission will help get you through it.

* * *

Upon arriving at a distance, the rumors begin to come true: this is one of the most beautiful places on Earth. Mountainous peaks come out of the water and are covered with palm trees in an immense jungle coming to the gentle ocean. The water and jungle are only separated by perfect, white, sandy beaches cascading into the clear blue water. Small wooden boats called long-tails are anchored to the beach one by one along a mile-long stretch of beach bars, clubs, and restaurants. Three-story dive boats milling about, moving to and from the docks and dive sites, transporting thousands of divers every day, are stretched across the landscape. It is time for some much-needed rest and relaxation after spending a couple years in a war zone. I am not aware of the challenging mission we are about to take on.

I am sitting in a dive instructor class of about fifteen, listening to legendary Mark Soworka talk about dive physics in Ko Tao, Thailand. Having taken the class once before, my mind begins to wander. "I've always wanted to break a world record," I think after browsing through an old bucket list I found. "What record could I break? I'm not exceptionally fast or strong." I begin searching the web for world records.

"A diving record?" I think to myself as I enter a search for scuba diving world records. The first page of results shows a list of records. The deepest dive was over three hundred meters, which sounded like certain death and years of training—no way. Longest dive, over a day underwater—that's not happening. Then I see it and nearly jump out of my seat in the middle of class.

A group of divers on an island called Utila in Honduras had built the largest underwater human pyramid during an annual festival with sixty-one people. Not many places host so many divers at one time, but on Koh Tao, one of the most active dive islands in the world, we might have a chance.

With the record in mind, I need support. Asking my cohort of dive instructor candidates if they wanted to participate is followed by immediate criticism. The idea is "too big," "People have tried," and "It'll never happen" is all I hear. Everyone has a lame excuse for being afraid to try, so I head home for the night, hoping my roommates are crazy enough to give it a shot.

"Are you serious? We can do that," John and Manolo say when I tell them the idea about breaking the record. "What do we need to get it done?" asks Manolo, an Army combat veteran I'd become friends with while becoming a scuba instructor in Thailand. "We'll need boats and equipment," John says in his Australian accent. "And we'll need divers, lots of divers," I reply as the three of us got to work laying out a plan.

"Yeah right—good luck," nearly everyone says in the beginning. Building early support is a challenge. After convincing our dive school to give us "the small boat" for the day, which could hold about twenty-five divers, we are able to get some much-needed practice at pyramid building. We convince only fifteen people in the first practice. When the first practice goes flawlessly, the fifteen people become microphones for the record. Our mission is spreading.

"Let's partner with the biggest dive schools for boats and equipment; maybe their divers will show up, too." We continue developing the plan over the next couple of weeks. "Let's get flyers out to every diver we know—the regulators can help get the word out. Who's submitting to Guinness?" After printing a map of all the dive schools on the island, I start driving around to find sponsors.

"We need your biggest boat for the day, all the scuba equipment needed to support that boat, and five hundred dollars," I say for possibly the seventieth time. "No, thank you, good luck," I hear again. Becoming fearful that we are running our companies to pitch, I wonder, "Will anyone support this?" I call John and Manolo to increase my morale after so much rejection; they try to set my mind at ease. "If it were easy, it wouldn't be a world record," they tell me lifting my spirits. "I'll get back on it tomorrow," I reply, packing it up for the day. Maybe tomorrow will be better.

I take a deep breath, opening the door to the largest dive school on the island named Ban's Dive Resort. "Sawadee krab" I say to the receptionist arriving inside of the AC-filled oasis shielding us from the intense tropical heat of August. "Is the manager available?"

Going through my presentation, I continue to show the manager our plan to break the record. She doesn't say a word, only motions me to continue. Finishing my presentation, I say again for almost the one hundredth time, "We need your biggest boat for the day, all the scuba equipment needed to support that boat, and five hundred dollars." She stares at me while a piece of sweat drips down my face. I expect the same reaction as I had gotten a hundred times before. "OK," she replies abruptly. It wasn't long after that we signed her rival company, Buddha View Dive Resort.

Two of the largest dive boats on the island connected to a bright orange buoy with a blue stripe and sit quietly waiting with nobody but the crew on board. Thirty feet underwater, a high-pitched horn squeals, and the hand signal is given. The sixty-two divers break apart from an underwater pyramid twenty-five feet tall into a storm of cheers, hugs, and acrobatic flips.

They all know the mission had been accomplished: the record has just been broken.[24]

Once we had a mission in mind, we were able to derive the components necessary to achieve the first. We were then able to identify the support we would need, rally our supporters, and maintain the perseverance necessary to get the resources.

---

24 (Guinness World Records, 2014)

Photo taken by Ban's Dive Resort, a sponsor of the World Record.

Becoming Your own Higher

"We service the friction points of the military journey," Sam Meek told me in an interview in his office, full of military memorabilia. The founder and CEO at Sandboxx, a fifty-plus employee tech start-up in Northern Virginia, had a lot to say about how their organization identifies, sets, and executes goals. His style of speaking and good nature immediately made me feel at ease.

"We have a lot of projects we want to try out. Most of our services, we've been focusing on first year of service," he told me about supporting this era of a soldier's life. Sam stood up, looking at the graph on the wall. Thinking about the service member's path as a whole, he began to narrow his view to specific points in time and pains that occur with each step. His intention is in "serving the friction points of the military journey."

"[For] example, when you go to boot camp, you don't have your phone with you, and that's a friction point." Sam continues the process to a specific problem. "So we built a letters platform," enabling friends and family of military members in bootcamp to send letters using an app integrating the tech environment with the postal service.

By identifying the problem they are trying to solve, the employees of Sandboxx continue to develop solutions in the form of actionable items. "You can get to 70 percent relatively quickly...by using that fail forward type of mantra but at the same time being very clear and articulate with the data." Sam sat back down and began flipping through a book.

"Like this book of all the letters you sent at bootcamp, after basic training. It's a cool product, but it hasn't been successful." He was unsure if they were going to keep the project going. "This is a great example of a project we spun up in two weeks and got this thing rolled out the door and started generating revenue within two weeks, and we may kill it."

Sam spoke very highly of the project and would like to keep it alive, but the company has to find a way for it to become profitable first. "We love the idea—we may figure out a way to keep it but nonetheless; it's something that we really believe in because we know a lot of families wanted some sort of keepsake for the letters they sent their loved ones in basic training."

Trial and error is important when trying to find your mission as well as the individual missions along the way to support your own vision as you become your own higher.

* * *

"I think about my mission as much as I can, on a daily basis," William Treseder told me over a phone call in early spring 2019. "I haven't made very good decisions in my life, when I've been thinking about huge, eternal, immortal, divine purpose."

"I usually use the distinction of uppercase P versus low-ercase p. Is it a big thing that doesn't change or a small thing that you do every day, that can change from day to day? I've been heavily influenced by the book, *Man's Search for Meaning* ," a book by Victor Frankl. Victor wrote a book after surviving the Holocaust.

In even the most treacherous of circumstances, the ability to find purpose in the little things can mean the difference between life and death. The small wins get you through the minute, the hour, and the day.

"He believes that, and it convinced me—that you should really focus on daily purpose and infusing significance in the small things you do every day and not try to create some big shiny purpose. For better or for worse, that's how I think about it." William's ability to focus on things he can control everyday sheds light on what he can be doing better now.

He can stop focusing so much on the "imagined place that you thought you were going to be." Forget the success and failure of some distant future goal and "focus a lot more on what you're doing today. Being a good citizen, and in my case, husband, father and boss. All the different things that I do every day, how am I living up to those things?" William tracks his progress of his daily wins with a checklist he completes each day.

"It feels very different than being a part of this big military apparatus where you can pat yourself on the back that you're making the world a safer place and nothing will ever live up to that, but I can still find a huge amount of satisfaction, and a different kind of satisfaction, in a more peaceful, contentment in doing really well every day," William said.

With the mission guiding your direction and finding accomplishment through daily action, soon you'll find others wanting to join the cause.

* * *

"When I joined the Marine Corps, I didn't want to kill and destroy—I wanted to defend," Rudy Reyes said. His training and experience in reconnaissance make him highly skilled as a contemporary warfighter. "This experience of life comes with a cost." Like a racehorse with no race, he had no mission.[25]

"If you know Rudy, he's like one of the fittest dudes on the planet. When I saw him, I could see it in his eyes that he was struggling." said Jim Ritterhoff, co-founder of Force Blue, during an interview. He was about to go diving down in the Cayman Islands, and he invited Rudy to come with. After ending their dives, Rudy told Jim, "This did more for me than any rehab, any therapy, or anything I've done since I've gotten out of the Marine Corps—we gotta get more of my guys here." He had found a way to use his advanced training for a new mission.

"Thank God I joined the Recon Marine and was mentored by the best men in the world," Rudy said, recalling his military training on an episode of *The Doctors*. "Combat water rescue swimmer, survival swimmer, and

---

25   (Reyes, 2018)

combat diver, and, with that prestigious knowledge, we learn about the ocean ourselves," Rudy continued, enumerating his dive-related skills that prepared him to complete his missions today.[26]

"We now created Force Blue, which parlays those skills to now fight in this battle to save the planet. We rebuild coral reefs around the world, we triage for diseased coral reefs. Now, we're involved with tagging sharks and turtles...protecting the blue, so we can have the green," Rudy said, naming the individual missions they are completing for their common goal. (Reyes, 2019)

"I had tangentially been involved on the environmental side," Jim said as he discussed the challenges of spreading the message for protecting the oceans and coral reefs. "What if we created a program that could help veterans identify mission in something bigger than themselves—mission therapy. Maybe in the process, reach a whole new audience that isn't going to listen to another climate change scientist but may listen to the Navy Seals, EOD, Marine Recon, or Air Force Para-Rescuemen, because the guys are their heroes."

26　(Reyes, 2019)

Rudy Reyes was in a dark place until he found his mission in an interesting way, enamored by the beauty of the underwater world. He developed this spark by bringing together combat divers to assist the fragile underwater world. Over time, his mission has grown, guiding the divers forward and sharing their passion with others as they continue to achieve missions.

Summary

Life is a spectrum of mission and depression. When humans have a mission, our choices are easier. We are guided by an overarching vision. The steps to get there are temporary, dynamic, and ever-changing. Some things will work, some things will not, but the mission will continue.

The distinction between the mission and missions—P vs p—along the way are important. This distinction is the essence of what Angela Duckworth's *Grit* is all about: devoting energy in one direction for a long time. The trial, error, success, and defeat of the missions along the way are what keeps the game moving in the direction and development of the mission.

As William adds, focusing on the daily actionable tasks that are actually performed is what enables him to remain gritty over time, to make micro-improvements and find happiness on the tactical level. The stakes are high, as the opposite end of the spectrum is depression. Explore to find a spark—it's hard to tell where it may come from.

* * *

- There exists a dichotomy between mission and depression. Moving toward one, moves you away from the other.
- Your highest-level goals give direction and must be developed over time into passion.
- Finding purpose in everyday tasks can lead to a happier life.
- Read *Grit* by Angela Duckworth.
- Think about your past experiences and identify themes and interests across your life.
- Make a list of ten daily tasks you want to improve upon each day and create a Google form for daily submissions

Chapter 4

Developing a Model

"The emergence of digital technologies has led to the rise of a digital economy which is impacting and transforming whole segments of industry especially the business models."[27]

Your Type of Business

Are you ready to start a business? Knowing the mission you are on is a start; now you must define the size and scope of the project and how it fits your currently desired lifestyle. As an example, let's go back to Thailand for a minute.

During my time in Thailand, I was fortunate enough to do hundreds of dives, including a somewhat misleadingly named one called a UV Night Dive, which really is blue light. It was like my first time diving again, shining

---

27   (Nwaiwu, 2018)

the light into the darkness underwater at night, trans-forming the reef into a fluorescent world never seen another way.

Over the next hour and a half, we don't leave a ten-by-ten-meter area. I shine the light in one area, and an eel comes swimming through the corals.

"An undulated eel!!" I mentally scream to myself in excitement.

This blackish-brown eel generally blends with the reef, making it hard to spot at night, but not on this dive. The eel is shining as yellow as the sun—against the dark backdrop, it was an easy find.

Everywhere I look, there are new creatures never seen on my dives before, glowing with beauty. The only way to explain it is like diving on acid. All the colors change, everything is glowing, and nothing looks like reality. I am blown away. "How do I get these lights?"

There is only one dive shop that was renting these lights on the island, and another one hundred-plus dive shops that didn't. I had already met them all from the world record and had an idea. What if I bought a few and offered them to everyone?

With a little digging, my friend Liam finds the manufacturer in Holland, and we place an order. I begin doing my rounds to all the dive shops for the second time.

It was an easy sell: "The other dive school on the island is charging fifty dollars more per dive with these lights and we charge no up-front cost to you—just call me when you have divers and I'll bring the lights down," I say to each dive school, leaving them a flyer I had made from a local graphic designer. It isn't long before the lights are completely rented out every night.

This business was very small. We take an order, deliver the lights, pick them up the next day, once per day, delivering to one or two dive shops.

That's when the problems begin. Receiving too many orders, we don't have enough lights, and my customers' unhappiness grows with the lights' unavailability. With only three months remaining of my time there, I have a decision to make: order more lights and grow the business or limit my sales to a key relationship. Knowing growth would require a lot more time and effort, I choose the latter, enjoying my much needed R&R while my housing costs were paid by my tiny little business. The month before I leave, I sell the business to my friend Ben, who is staying around longer.

Knowing key life events were going to change and this business wasn't for the long-term helped drive the kind of business I wanted for my life at the time: I had a choice, and I could only choose one. It became an overall enjoyable experience.

* * *

There are three types of business: salary substitute, lifestyle. and entrepreneurial, according to research done by Poposka, Navevski & Mihajlovsk.[28]

1. Salary Substitute: "Micro enterprises which offer common products or services to consumers by providing their owner with a regular paycheck."[29]
2. Lifestyle businesses: "Enable the entrepreneur to pursue his dreams by making a living out of his/hers hobbies." [30] Not only does the business provide a paycheck, but it also enables the owner the freedom to explore the lifestyle they desire.
3. Entrepreneurial businesses: "Breaks the system of equilibrium by introducing new combinations to the market."[31] As we'll see later, this type is where

---

28 (Poposka, Nanevski and Mihajlovska, 2019)

29 (Poposka, Nanevski and Mihajlovska, 2019)

30 (Poposka, Nanevski and Mihajlovska, 2019)

31 (Poposka, Nanevski and Mihajlovska, 2019)

the unicorns and the woodpeckers live: a place of innovation, growth, and challenges all their own. These businesses are the arena where many people I've interviewed work and live, but it's not the only way.

My childhood in the Midwest was surrounded by mom-and-pop small businesses starting up to fill a local need or service. My father started a salary substitute business, installing flooring as an independent contractor and eventually growing enough to build his own team and several teams that service a more than one hundred-mile area. Like any business, these businesses can flourish and grow, providing the owner and their employees a potential lifetime of employment and financial security. If the business is your passion or dream, it begins crossing over to a lifestyle business.

After planting his roots in paradise, Jeremie Green began starting several lifestyle businesses, enabling himself to live where he wants and do the work he finds fun and interesting. He identifies businesses tourists would enjoy and then goes and builds them.

His newest development is a three-story water slide that launches people into the pool of his club. "I'm from South Florida—we do pool parties. We wanted to build something that wasn't just a slide attraction, but was a venue." Jeremie has utilized his businesses as a form of self-expression and enjoyment while supporting his tourist niche. "We saw that there was a void missing from other slide projects around the world that we could correct and fix."

While travel is not required to meet the definition of a lifestyle business, meeting digital nomads around the world has opened my eyes to this attractive option. In the digital world, specific locations and times are no longer a requirement. Those people who learn how to harness this power may find themselves living in multiple counties following the sun or working from their perfect hideaway.

Defining the type of business you are about to create will assist you in developing a model that achieves your personal and business goals. Becoming the next Facebook doesn't have to be your first endeavor. No matter the style or size of business you would like to create, experimenting will be crucial in every mission you create along the way.

Developing a Model

"The concept of business models generally refers to the architecture of a business or the way a firm structures its activities in order to create and capture value for itself."[32] Business models, like a mission, are honed and evolve.

"In any given industry, a dominant business model tends to emerge over time. In the absence of market distortions, the model will reflect the most efficient way to allocate and organize resources."[33] As new combinations and ideas become available, new models will challenge the old.

It is the business model rather than the technology that enables and creates the disruptive effect.[34] Facebook didn't invent photo sharing or messaging: it combined them together into a new format that people loved.

Like Sam Meek and his team at Sandboxx connecting an app to the postage system, Facebook developed an early model and found ways to expand its model over time. Finding a workable model that aligns with reality is the real challenge.

---

32 (Nwaiwu, 2018)
33 (Kavadias, Ladas and Loch, 2016)
34 (Christensen, 1997)

Steve Blank identified two key points when giving a lecture about the principles of lean. "Start-ups are not smaller versions of large companies." Large companies execute known business models, which is how they got large. "Start-ups search for unknown business models."[35]

To *find* the right fit, many models will have to be developed, tested, and improved. "If you really think about it, a business plan, makes all the sense in the world for your second, third, fifth product in a large corporation—because you have a series of knowns." Steve says.[36]

"In a start-up, you don't have a series of knowns—you have a series of unknowns," Steve continues. Different tools will have to be used in a start-up, and they have now expanded to large corporations and government.[37]

Creating Value:
The business model canvas has been designed to "map, discuss, design and invent new business models."[38] The canvas is broken up into nine segments that cover all

35   (Blank, 2016)
36   (Blank, 2016)
37   (Blank, 2016)
38   (Strategizer, 2011)

aspects of the business model to be developed and iterated upon.

The first time I actually sat down and forced myself to create a business model, I had a real challenge. It was hard for me to know where to start. How could *I* create value in a differentiated way?

Fortunately, I was already passionate about finance and entrepreneurship, so I had a starting point. After finding the business model canvas, my understanding of what was important in business planning changed.

Utilizing this framework, entrepreneurs can quickly design a multitude of business models, combine them, add pieces, remove pieces, and play around imagining things not thought of before. The nine segments come together as a model.

Who, What, and Where:

The business model starts with the customer who will receive the value you create. A value proposition then matches your products and services to their problems and desires. Once the mechanism to create value is identified, determining where to deliver the value is described in the channels and followed by defining the type of relationship to be developed with the customer. Finally, figuring out the money flow sheds light on the potential revenue of each model.[39]

1. **Customer Segments:** personas of who is using your product/service. "If you're a newspaper company, you have two segments; the reader, and the advertisers that want to reach the readers," Alex Osterwalder said.[40]

2. **Value Proposition**: The value proposition identifies how your products and services solve customer problems and improve their lives. Matching the correct combination of products and services that solve the customer's problems is what creates value.[41]

3. **Channels:** "How do my customers want to be reached?" Alex asks describing the channels of a business. The channel is where you interact with your customers. They are the "touch-points" of interacting and delivering value. [42]

4. **Customer Relationships:** Depending on the type of company or customer, your relationship may be through a website, in-person, an app, or any other combination that could be developed. The type of

---

39 (Osterwilder, 2012)
40 (Osterwalder, 2012)
41 (Osterwalder, 2012)
42 (Osterwilder, 2012)

relationship will dictate the roles needed to provide the product or service.[43]

5. **Revenue Streams:** the mechanism for capturing value. "What are people really willing to pay for?" Alex asks. Are customers purchasing a subscription, a fee, or does a third-party pay you? Revenue streams define what exchange takes place and where. What is the pathway the money will take from the customer to your business?[44]

How You Do It:

Determining who, what, and where you're going to provide your product or service happens first, then you begin to identify the resources, activities, partnerships, and costs.

1. **Key Resources:** the infrastructure to create, deliver, and capture value. You will also identify which assets are indispensable and which are simply wasteful spending.[45]

2. **Key Activities:** the things your business must do well. Knowing what you do informs you of what you have to do well as a company. This key activity is your specialty and must be developed as well as

---

43 (Osterwalder, 2012)

44 (Osterwalder, 2012)

45 (Osterwalder, 2012)

your training in the military. "What is it we really do?" Alex asks. "Do I write it, do I market, do I sell?" he continues. You must determine which pieces of the puzzle is your piece to solve.[46]

3. **Key Partnerships:** Business relationships can enhance your product or service. Who can help you leverage your business model? "A lot of the new business models are partnerships," Alex says. No business is built alone or in isolation. We need "air support." Who are the other experts that can provide services and assistance where you cannot?[47]

4. **Cost Structure:** Upon completing the key resources, key activities, and key partnerships, the costs are derived and the cost structure is created. Every dollar spent is a choice away from one opportunity to try another. All cost must now be added to define the cost of delivering the value.[48]

With a new business model in hand, the potential revenue from creating value is measured against the cost of creating the value. If the model creates value, it may be worth pursuing. After multiple models have been created, they can then be compared with each other and the optimal model chosen to test.

---

46 (Osterwalder, 2012)
47 (Osterwalder, 2012)
48 (Osterwalder, 2012)

Build Multiple Models

Is your first idea usually your best? Not likely. Taking the time using a creative process to develop multiple models will generate new ideas not thought of on the first attempt. Ideas will lead to other ideas and can be sifted through and rearranged as the model develops. Enlist in others for feedback or assistance in creating the model to spark new ideas.

Start combining parts of models together into combinations that may or may not survive further development. This process sheds light on what you know and, maybe more importantly, *what you don't know.*

After completing a few models, review the resource needs of each and prioritize the list from best to worst. It's time to start gathering intel: everything we know up to this point is unconfirmed.

Test

"You know nothing, John Snow," says Ygritte in the famous line from *Game of Thrones*, summarizing the knowledge an entrepreneur has after inventing a business model from thin air. Our ideas must be tested against reality.

"How many entrepreneurs have tested their business models before they built it?" asked Alex Osterwalder. Ideas are great, but they often don't represent reality. "Most business plans don't survive the first customer contact," Alex says. Like the mission plan on the battlefield, first enemy contact will destroy any plans.[49]

Summary

Knowing the size and type of business you want to build to support your lifestyle is an important first step. Look inward to find what you want.

Then, searching for the appropriate product or service to deliver requires experimentation, the starting point being an exercise to develop multiple models using the nine segments on Strategyzer's Business Model Canvas. The models are developed, chopped up, rearranged, pieced back together, and reviewed for value creation.

Using this process will enable you to rapidly develop models that can be tested in reality for the correct fit. As new data becomes available, the model is updated with this new knowledge, attempting to align with an ever-moving target.

---

49   (Osterwalder, 2012)

Taking a scientific approach removes the threat of "failure" and transforms it into an exploration of the real world and the economy.

* * *

- Five Ms of starting a movement: Message, Messenger, (Wo)Manpower, Machine, and Momentum
- There are three types of business: salary substitute, lifestyle, and entrepreneurial. Each requires different skills and models.
- A business model describes how you create and capture value.
- Business models drive innovation.
- Build multiple business models first, then start testing.
- Think about something important enough to start a movement.
- Think about three ways you could create a business for each type of business.
- Review the Business Model Canvas by Strategyzer.
- Read Business Model Generation and Value Proposition Design from the Strategyzer Series.

Chapter 5

Agile Thinking

"But mouse-friend, you are not alone in proving fore-sight may be vain: the best-laid schemes of Mice and Men, go oft awry, and leave us only grief and pain, for promised joy!"[50]

"When you go out, every time you're scared," Raymond Lott said, recounting his time in Iraq as a combat correspondent—essentially a combat journalist. "I was just like anybody; you didn't even know the difference except I had a camera around my neck."

Moving around with units on the battlefield, Raymond's job is to document the battlefield so others would know what happened. "They're just like, go write stories and take photos."

---

50   (Burns and Burch, n.d.)

His most important piece of kit is his five thousand dollar camera, and that day he has a problem: his camera is broken. If you've been in the military, you know breaking a piece of critical kit can have consequences.

"Hey Gunny, I broke my camera," he says, not knowing the response he will receive. "You did what?!?!" his Gunnery Sergeant responds, followed by a reprimand. "You better figure it out!" he says, finishing his rant abruptly turning and walking away with intent. "I will, Gunny—the next photo I take is gonna be amazing," Raymond yells to his distant superior.

Needing to figure out his situation without many options, he pulls two hundred dollars from the ATM and buys a point-and-shoot camera. Raymond gears up, taking out the multiple lenses from his drop pouch and replacing them with a single item, his new basic camera. The team heads out on patrol.

"I come around the corner of a building, and I see the most beautiful girl in the world," Raymond told me. "We both looked at each other." Surprised she doesn't have her face covered, he raises his new camera up and snaps a photo.

"That photo won the best photo of the military in 2006," Raymond said nonchalantly.

Not all encounters overseas are treacherous—there are great people around the world are trying to survive and live their lives in peace. After the photo, she serves them Naan and tea, a custom in the area for hospitality.

Leadership in the military forces you to overcome and find a way to solve problems. Not always having the right tools, we must be adaptable, do more with less, and make it happen either way.

In the future, when Raymond becomes the CEO of a record label, he will once again need these adaptive skills to overcome the challenges before him when the situation doesn't go as planned.

Testing Ideas in Uncertainty

In an uncertain world, we must be flexible. Disarming bombs, we dealt with a lot of uncertainty. Many of the bombs we worked on in the field were called Improvised Explosive Devices (IEDs). As the name implies, they can be made up of anything and are, quite literally, up to the human imagination. Since this is the case, it's not really effective to develop a detailed plan of what's going to happen. Instead, we need to be extremely prepared in our training, proficient in our tools, and have the ability to be present in the moment harnessing skills to dynamically adapt to an ever-changing environment.

One day back in Afghanistan in 2008, we are clearing the only road in and out of Korengal Valley. "The Valley of Death," and its people have a long history of fighting any outsider daring enough to enter without permission. Even the locals heed the warning.

"As a particularly isolated and independent tribe, the Korengalis weren't used to having outsiders in their valley. They speak their own particular dialect of Pashto and had managed to keep both the Taliban and the Soviets out."[51]

It hasn't gotten any better. We all know the risk every time we go, but there is a small base at the top of the valley and the soldiers need food, water, and basic necessities of life. The locals won't deliver the supplies unless the route is cleared in front of them. It's going to be a long day.

---

51   (Hetherington, 2011)

The road is a little over six miles. At our best approximation, this trek will take us twelve hours, if all goes right. We set off from FOB Asadabad at 5:00 a.m. to arrive at the valley at sunrise. Not long after, we're taking a left across the bridge and enter the mouth of the Korengal with towering peaks steeply rising on each side. We drive straight into the belly of the beast.

We're expecting to get shot at, we're expecting to get blown up, and, most of all, we're deathly afraid of rolling our truck off the cliff as the road crumbles a bit beneath the weight of our vehicle. The thirty thousand pounds of metal and bulletproof glass on a road just barely wide enough for your tires to be right on the edge of the cliff.

On an earlier occasion to the Korengal, we had a close call when the back left tire of the rear vehicle slides off the edge of the cliff. Narrowly escaping a rollover, we recover the vehicle with tow straps.

"You've got at least six inches on this side, plenty of room," I tell my teammate Mike over the radio while looking over the edge of the gunner's turret down at the road. My stomach churns a bit as I try to avoid looking down the three hundred-meter cliff, beginning just beyond where our tires end.

I take a deep breath as we pass over the most narrow section; many in the convoy dismount and prefer to take the rest of the trip by foot to avoid the possibility of a rollover.

We're nearly there. Everyone is in fairly high spirits, and we close upon the top of Korengal Valley with no incident. "Hopefully, we'll get some chow soon," I think to myself as sweat drips across my glasses."

Some of our security begin grouping together while walking on the road. "Hey, y'all trying to get blown up together? Maybe you should spread out!" our team leader Mick announces in his Southern accent over the loudspeaker to our engineer and security team becoming complacent in front of us after an already long journey.

"Maybe you morons want to walk on the mountain instead of the road?" He continues mocking them over the loudspeaker, half joking but deadly serious.

BOOOM! Metal goes flying all around, bouncing off the vehicle while a fireball erupts from the road one hundred meters ahead of us at a curve in the road. Our lead vehicle flies ten feet in the air and comes crashing down to the ground, all of its wheels and axles completely removed.

We watch the troops on the ground only twenty meters from the blast scramble to the hills.

VIC 4: "Vic 1, Vic 4, what's your situation?"

VIC 1: The radio is silent for a few seconds, which seem like an eternity.

VIC 4: VIC: "Vic 1, Vic 4, how copy?"

Silence.

VIC 4: "Vic 1, Vic 4, what is your situation?"

VIC 1: "Vic 4, this is Vic 1, these motherfuckers blew up my truck."

Everyone sighs in relief to hear the lead vehicle joking about getting blown up for the third time on this deployment.

What about the dismounted troops? All soldiers begin checking in to provide their situation.

Fortunately, for the dismounted troops, a large boulder deflected the blast as the explosion happened around the corner, narrowly avoiding several "Killed in Action."

Happy we have no casualties, our EOD team gets to work.

We clear the scene and make sure the area is safe. Around 5:00 p.m., we have to solve our final problem: how do we get the lead vehicle back to base? With the wheels blown off, the vehicle is the shape of a plow, and we're 5.5 miles into Korengal Valley. We've been in the valley about nine hours, and, the longer we stay, the more time the enemy has to prepare an attack, and it's going to get dark soon.

We get together to come up with possible solutions. "Can we get a recovery vehicle up here? Helicopter? What if we pull it out, we might tear up the road but could we do it?" We throw ideas back and forth. "Let's try to pull it first—we can try that now while we identify other resources," someone suggests.

"OK, let's go." We begin positioning the vehicles and connecting tow straps.

As we begin pulling the vehicle, there is almost an immediate ninety-degree turn to the right in the road. As the tow vehicle takes the corner, the angle of pull changes and starts pulling the vehicle towards the edge of the cliff.

Soon the front of the vehicle is hanging over the cliff, within five minutes, we knew this plan would not work. We get back together.

"Any update on the helicopter?" we ask the commander. "They don't have the right assets, we have to find another way," he responds, ending any chances of flying this thing out of the valley. "It's close to the cliff, can we push it off?" We keep discussing options.

"You've got approval to push this thing off the mountain—we'll start pulling everything out of the vehicle," says the commander. Using our rear bumper, I align it with the front of the mangled vehicle, and I start pushing on the gas. The sounds of metal on metal fill the air as the tires spin, trying to grip the road.

Leaving my door open in case I need to bail, I look at the back of the vehicle and my tires spinning.

"This isn't going to work—I can barely move this thing, and when it goes, I don't want to go with it," I yell to our team lead. "We've got C4; let's blow this thing off the mountain. Can we get approval?" Mike adds.

"What's taking so long?" we ask over our internal comms while sitting in the truck pulling security. Our NVGs are on to see in the completely dark valley, except for a couple of fires in the distance.

Curing our hunger while taking turns pulling security in the gun turret, we eat some Ottis Spunkmeyer muffins and wash it down with a nice cold Rip It. The blue Rip Its are the best. The others catching a nap in preparation for the work ahead.

"EOD, we've got approval," the commander calls over the radio.

Hours had gone by since we had tried to push the vehicle off the cliff. It's too heavy, but we have one final hope.

"We've got four cases—keep one in case we need it," my team lead yells out. "I hope it will be enough," I respond back. Mike and I start prepping everything and looking at each other with excitement.

"I can't believe we get to blow this up off the mountain!" he says, laughing. "We've got the best job in the military," I reply, grinning.

"Fire in the hole, fire in the hole, fire in the hole., Mike yells, pulling the ring on the initiator.

BOOM! The valley lights up as a fireball emerges from the darkness. The vehicle is thrown in the air and comes crashing back down on the road. "I hope it moved enough—we don't have enough C to try again," Mick says as the night returns to darkness.

"We'll have just enough room to get by," Mick calls over the radio. "Good work, y'all."

Operating in such a challenging environment leads to complex situations. The right tools are rarely available, and, sometimes, trial and error is the only approach. When trial and error is the necessary methodology like in entrepreneurship, learning quickly what will and won't work happens through experimentation. When a test becomes too high-risk, other strategies must be developed.

Experimentation

"If it disagrees with experiment, it's wrong. In that simple statement, is the key to science." –Richard Feynman

Feynman, a legendary Nobel Prize-winning physicist, described the scientific method in a lecture. "First, we guess it." The standing room-only student audience erupts laughing. "Don't laugh, it's really true," he retorted without missing a beat. Stressing the importance of this stage in the process, he declared, "It's...not unscientific to take a guess." A guess is only a hypothesis, however, and the hypothesis must be testable.[52]

"Then we compute the consequences of the guess to see [what it would imply]." The guess must have consequences—it will establish a definable consequence. The defined consequences can then be tested to verify their agreement with the world. (Feynman, n.d.)

"Then we compare those computation results to nature, or we can say to experiment or experience." Feynman said, walking back and forth between the podium and the chalkboard. "If it disagrees with experiment, it's wrong. In that simple statement is the key to science." But does that make it right? No.[53]

---

52 (Feynman, n.d.)
53 (Feynman, n.d.)

"In the future, you could create a wider arrangement of experiments, a wider arrangement of consequences, and you may discover that this thing is wrong." Feynman suggest that the known information is only as good as our ability to predict its outcomes. These principles were incorporated into manufacturing by Toyota in the 1980s and have exploded across business in the form of Agile and Lean development. If the scientist figured out the process so long ago, why has it taken business so long to catch on? In an ever-changing world of uncertainty, we don't have time to be slow to adapt. (Feynman, n.d.)

Starting Lean

"Within my first year, I started my first business in September of 2009," Taylor Justice told me in an interview.

"My mentor at West Point, a guy named Joe Ross—he was the director at a program called the Center for Enhanced Performance...we were both medically discharged at the same time," Taylor continued. The program was about peak performance and the moderators believed they could "flip it on it's head" and begin training corporate America. They began building a team: Higher Echelon was born.

Identifying another 1995 West Point graduate for their team, they began building the program. "Joe built the resilient and adaptable leader program, and we started to sell it." Taylor casually lists some of their clients. "We started to sell it to eBay, PayPal, Merck Pharmaceuticals; MIT started teaching this leadership course and then it started evolving into this government contracting business." The business was beginning to pivot.

Joe moved to Huntsville, Alabama, home of Redstone Arsenal and host of my predeployment EOD training. "We really started to grind it out and build relationships," something Taylor experienced in his first job. In Taylor's first job, he learned the skills of selling in front of an audience.

He had a realization. "I'm selling something right now, and the only difference is, I'm doing it for a big corporation."

For the next five years, he would work part-time putting his sales skills to work building Higher Echelon.

"I worked part-time for five years....It wasn't until two or three years with Joe, until we had enough revenue where Joe could go full-time, and eventually Paul went full-time." Taylor and his team were bootstrapping the business until it could afford to pay them full-time, and now they have over one hundred employees.

Closing his chapter with Higher Echelon, Taylor had a new mission to accomplish. "I left Higher Echelon officially in 2014—that's when Unite Us was really ramping up. It was time for him to pivot again and focus on a new start-up, this time to fill his guilty void of service after being medically discharged from a training accident. His unit went on without him, and some of them didn't come back.

* * *

Start-up: a human institution designed to deliver a new product or service under conditions of uncertainty."[54]

Why do so many startups fail?" aska Eric Ries, author *of The Lean Startup.* "We're building products that nobody wants."[55]

Business owners take a guess at what their customers want, build the product, and try to sell it. He calls this "successfully achieving failure, which is, when you suc-

---

54   (Ries, 2010)
55   (Ries, 2010)

cessfully execute a plan straight off a cliff." Changing our point of view can improve our odds of success.[56]

"We're taking untested, unvalidated assumptions and we are pouring people's time and energy into them." Eric described the typical start-up today. Shifting our mind-set to a scientific method of hypothesizing, testing, measuring, and iterating is what he suggests.[57] Maybe then we'd have a chance at succeeding.

Eric posed the question, "Not only can we build a product, but should we?" Just because we can make something, and we think it's a good idea, doesn't mean we'll be right.[58]

Especially the first time we try. The world is too complex and dynamic. We must seek to *learn* what the market wants through experimentation and have the flexibility to pivot: "change directions but stay grounded in what we've learned."[59]

Lean Startup provides a framework to operate in an unknown universe.

---

56 (Ries, 2010)
57 (Ries, 2010)
58 (Ries, 2010)
59 (Ries, 2010)

"The unknown problem, unknown solution" is the universe the start-up lives. The problem, solution, and even customer may not be known and must be tested via "Validated Learning."[60]

"Build Measure Learn" is the process Eric suggests. "We take vision, we turn it into action, through that action we reveal the truth about our vision and we iterate." It is only after we have tested it that we know reality supports it.[61]

The key is to start small. Eric spent six months writing 40,000 lines of for a project he worked on to learn this concept. They project developers built a program that was "as likely to crash your computer as it was to work," as Eric puts it. When they released, nobody downloaded it.[62]

He wonders how fast he could have learned the same information without writing 40,000 lines of code. "Could I have learned it with 20,000 lines of code? 10,000? What if I had just asked some customers if they would like to download this program? Would I have

60   (Ries, 2010)
61   (Ries, 2010)
62   (Ries, 2010)

learned the same amount in one week that I had learned in six months?"[63]

He could have started first by finding a product idea customers wanted to download then building iterations of the product, releasing them incrementally and identifying measurable outcomes to make choices in the next iteration.

"*The Lean Startup* method is not about cost; it is about speed." How quickly can you come up with an idea, find a way to test it, and measure the outcomes to create improvements?[64]

* * *

"Plans are worthless, but planning is everything." Jeff Sutherland quoted President Dwight Eisenhower in a TedX talk. "When I got to be a fighter pilot, I was in reconnaissance, we did a lot of planning." Jeff continued to tell a story about fighting in Vietnam.[65]

"But one day, one of my fellow pilots, Ed Adderberry, was blown out of the sky by a SAM missile....He did

---

63 (Ries, 2010)

64 (Ries, 2010)

65 (Sutherland, 2014)

good planning, but was flying low and level over the target." Jeff describes the "lessons learned" he took from the ultimate sacrifice of his brother on the battlefield.[66][67]

"My plan was to have a vision where the target was and as soon as I crossed North Vietnam, I went into an evasive maneuver because every second I knew I was being fired at." Jeff described his flight pattern on missions starting the day after Ed was shot down. "And only at the last second would I come up, straight and level off, just for a second to snap the photo." Flying reconnaissance missions was a dangerous endeavor.[68]

"I got out alive, but nearly half the people I flew with didn't come back from their missions." Jeff was fortunate to survive those dangerous times, and rapidly adapting to the battlefield surely played a role in his survival. He later adapted these skills to business developing a new system of teamwork.[69]

"When I came back to the United States, it was a big surprise. I had come so close to getting killed so many

---

66 (Sutherland, 2014)
67 (Pownetwork.org.,1990)
68 (Sutherland, 2014)
69 (Sutherland, 2014)

times—it was like a new life. Every day was like a new day, a bonus day," Jeff said.[70]

Jeff became driven by passion, and, eventually, the lessons he learned at the Army Academy, in war, and his professional life led him to co-develop Scrum, a framework of adaptive development, a way to implement ideas on a team. Although these skills are ingrained in us in the military, adapting them to business takes new training.

Scrum

Scrum: a framework within which people can address complex adaptive problems while productively and creatively delivering products of the highest possible value.[71]

"The essence of Scrum is a small team of people," says *The Scrum Guide* (TSG), created by Ken Schwaber and Jeff Sutherland. These teams self-organize and self-manage to create at a rapid pace. The process has a strong feeling of military mission planning, likely influenced

---

70   (Sutherland, 2014)
71   (Schwaber and Sutherland, 2017)

by Jeff's time in the Army Academy and as a pilot in Vietnam.[72]

"Scrum employs an iterative, incremental approach to optimize predictability and control risk." (TSG) Scrum advises creating bite-sized tasks to be completed in one– to four-week periods of time, followed by improvements of successive periods.[73]

"The individual team is highly flexible and adaptive." These teams operate individually and together with other teams to complete tasks, features, projects, products, and programs.[74]

The main event of the Scrum is the sprint, the one– to four-week period of time the development team has to create the deliverable product. Supported by the Scrum Master, the Development Team continues completing tasks self-selected from a prioritized list selected before the Sprint. The team creates the deliverable *without interruption* during the designated period.[75]

---

72 (Schwaber and Sutherland, 2017)

73 (Schwaber and Sutherland, 2017)

74 (Schwaber and Sutherland, 2017)

75 (Schwaber and Sutherland, 2017)

In the previous paragraph, I mentioned a few of the key players involved in scrum. They are the Product Owner, Development Team, and Scrum Master. I'll briefly review each of their roles and responsibilities.

- **"The Product Owner** is responsible for maximizing the value of the product resulting from work of the Development Team." (TSG) The Product Owner develops a master list prioritizing functionalities and capabilities to be created for released called the Priorities Backlog List (PBL).[76]
- **The Development Team** is a small team of three to nine "professionals who do the work of delivering a potentially releasable Increment of 'Done' product at the end of each Sprint." This group should be able to complete their own tasks and work. "They are self-organizing. No one (not even the Scrum Master) tells the Development Team how to turn Product Backlog into Increments of potentially releasable functionality." They are responsible for the Sprint Backlog List. (SBL)[77]
- **"The Scrum Master** is a servant-leader for the Scrum Team. The Scrum Master helps those outside the Scrum Team understand which of their interactions with the Scrum Team are helpful and which

---

76 (Schwaber and Sutherland, 2017)
77 (Schwaber and Sutherland, 2017)

aren't." They support the entire team, including the Product Owner, Development Team, and Organization, always promoting a functional Scrum Team by removing barriers and protecting the team from unnecessary external elements.[78]

The team gathers together to plan the Sprint, a "time-box" of one month or less to complete the releasable product iteration. The team creates a Sprint Goal, and the development team chooses tasks from the PBL to accomplish during the Sprint. "The entire Scrum Team collaborates on understanding the work of the Sprint," states TSG. The team does enough planning to estimate how much can be accomplished during the sprint. Blocks of time are added to the calendar for each item on the PBL, creating a new list called the Sprint Backlog List. The SBL is made by the Development Team and no others have a say in the list. With the SBL finalized, the Sprint begins.[79]

Each day, at the same time and place, there is a "15-minute time-boxed event for the Development Team" called the Daily Scrum. The team members review progress and discusses how they will work towards achieving the Sprint Goal that day. Ask, "What did I do yesterday...?",

---

78   (Schwaber and Sutherland, 2017)
79   (Schwaber and Sutherland, 2017)

"What will I do today...?", and "Do I see any impediments...?" all with the Sprint Goal in mind, says TSG.

The team members review the SBL and their progress to completion. The Scrum Master is around to facilitate and ensure the teams have their meetings. The Daily Scrum is an internal meeting to the Development Team, except for the Scrum Master and non interrupting visitors.[80]

The team works together to complete the SBL containing the tasks of the Sprint. They add to and take away from the SBL as tasks are completed or generated by the Development Team to achieve the Sprint Goal, checking in every day at the Daily Scrum and tracking progress to the goal.[81]

Similar to an after-action report, upon completion of the Sprint, the Scrum Team and stakeholders conduct a Sprint Review and Retrospective. They discuss what happened during the sprint, what was completed and any changes to the PBL during the review, how the last sprint went, major items that went well, and anything

---

80   (Schwaber and Sutherland, 2017)
81   (Schwaber and Sutherland, 2017)

that could improve in the next sprint. "The Scrum Master encourages the team to improve."[82]

At the end of a Sprint, the team should have achieved a product "increment," "A body of inspectable, done work that supports empiricism at the end of the Sprint." The product should be a finished product that the product owner "may choose to immediately release." Once one Sprint is complete, the process begins again with Sprint Planning.[83]

The scrum guide and other similar tools provide a framework of experimentation in business. Applying these tools like a military member would apply mission planning improved outcomes over time through validated learning.

Summary

The world is uncertain and so is business. You must utilize frameworks to assist you in comparing your ideas to reality. Starting with the idea of applying the scientific method, you can incorporate the The Business Model Canvas, *Lean Startup*, and Scrum into your daily activities.

---

82   (Schwaber and Sutherland, 2017)
83   (Schwaber and Sutherland, 2017)

Using these tools, you can begin to design methods to test your ideas, eventually leading to the creation of an idea that is in line with nature and the current state in the world. Remain agile in your thinking and pivot quickly when new information becomes available.

* * *

- Be flexible and do more with less.
- War and entrepreneurship are worlds of uncertainty.
- *Lean*, agile, and scrum principles are useful to test ideas and measure for results.
- Read *The Lean Startup* and *The Scrum Guide*
- Utilize the Business Model Canvas and *The Scrum Guide* to develop a minimal, viable product action plan.
- Conduct your first Sprint.

Chapter 6

Missions

"Oh, man. Planning, planning, planning, planning: the orders process for officers. Holy shit, if you actually study it, and embrace it, and make an effort to be great at it...you'll be set up for success for the rest of your life," Donny O'Malley said in our interview. He was referring to the USMC Officer Orders process.

The process begins by orienting yourself to your environment, defining your mission, and developing the "how-to" and contingencies. Planning is done at every level of the organization and kept down to five paragraphs: Situation, Mission, Execution, Administration and Logistics, and Command and Signal.

Failed Orientation

After three months at sea, sailing from China past South America, I arrive in Cancun. The beach chairs had arrived. I am living in Playa del Carmen, Mexico, a fantastic place of beautiful culture, immense jungle, historic ruins, and the world-famous cenotes. These sites drive thousands of tourists from all over the world to visit. One of the most visited sights is the white, sandy beaches of Mexico's Gulf coastline. All this coastline, and not a single place selling beach chairs. I see an opportunity and order a container from China off the website Alibaba, essentially the Amazon of Chinese manufacturing.

"Yo tengo un negocio aqui con sillas de playa para rentar," I explain to the managers in Spanish. I am not fluent, but have to learn quickly—our partner who was local to Mexico had bailed on the project just a couple days before the container arrived. My other partner Mo and I have to speak with lawyers, accountants, and government officials; not all of them speak English.

Thinking about my success in Thailand by partnering with many organizations to offer my product, we go looking for partners. For days and days, we present our business partnership agreement to the local vendors and hotels, and many agree. Excited to have our product in over thirty locations, we are ready for the surge of customers and the steady cash flow that comes with it.

The phone never rings.

The tourists don't care about our product. The sales people just go on with business as usual, not even mentioning our program. The river of people flooding down the main tourist walkway, 5th Avenue, are too busy looking at all the local displays of art and trinkets to even notice our advertisements.

"They've swapped out our flyer?" I think to myself in disgust as I look at a stand from a distance while walking down 5th to check in with the seven vendors we're partnered with. They had replaced our beach chair flyer with a tour they were selling. We don't have the sales staff buy-in, and the project is going too long without success. We try to sell them to hotels, Airbnbs, friends, vacation rentals, everywhere—with only a few sales.

"We've gotta shut it down, Mo," I say to my partner. "This project is a bust." With only days left before shipping the entire load back to Cancun, I begin venting my frustrations and desperation to Mo.

"I'm loading up the tricycle and just driving down 5th," I tell Mo, thinking about getting directly in front of the tourists. With only ten days left, I open the garage door to our Airbnb, which is packed full of boxes and a tricycle. Peddling off, I take a left to head toward 5th

Avenue. I pedal slowly, casually asking people if they need a beach chair as I roll by.

A local approaches me and asks me a question or two in Spanish about the chairs. Doing my best to communicate, we cordially part ways, which is customary in the local community. Two blocks further and I'm on 5th Avenue; it's early morning so the river of people has trickled down to a bubbling brook. Another local approaches me. Telling him the chairs are for sale, he pulls out some money and buys one. He takes the chair back to his taxi stand where five others are lounging on the ground.

Soon the others take notice and come rushing up to the tricycle. The rush of hands paying money and grabbing chairs was almost hard to track it was happening so fast. The tricycle was sold out in about ten minutes. Turning back, I load up again, and again, and again, selling over seventy chairs that day.

It is too late. We spend the remaining days going around town, even renting a van for a day to go to Tulum and other locations outside of Playa. We sell what we could, pay the employees, and shut the door.

Had we taken more time to orient ourselves to the environment to see who were the true players, we might have succeeded. Missions go wrong when they are not properly oriented, when the players involved are not understood, and when you don't understand the business environment. Preparing and planning for these variables takes time and energy; failing to understand can cost even more.

Prior to planning the mission, we hadn't properly oriented ourselves. We had a hypothesis but realized too late that the locals were, in fact, our customers for transportable, comfortable seating. We could have learned this more quickly, and cheaply, by taking a trip to Mexico and trying to sell the container before we ordered it to identify interest in the need. We would have learned more about the local area and maybe even found a product the hotel partnerships wanted to order. Get out and speak with everyone involved in your mission space.

Orientation Paragraph

"Prior to issuing an order, the unit leader orients his subordinate leaders to the planned area of operation using a terrain model, map, or when possible, the area of operation."[84] Who are the forces at play? Are the players known?

Are they friendly to your cause or unfriendly in some way? What advantages do you have and what advantages do they have? How does the environment in which interaction takes place affect the players? These are only some of the questions that need to be answered to be properly oriented.

"A leader's reconnaissance is arranged to confirm the unit leader's estimate of the situation."[85] Your assumptions must be confirmed.

Analyze your opponent. Who is competing with you in the same mission space? Determine their size and capabilities. Where are they going, and why are they going there? This includes the competition, suppliers, allies, and customers. The more information that can be obtained, the clearer the image of the environment will be. You have to get out there and see it for yourself.

Of course, events don't happen in a vacuum, and all of these components will be dynamically engaging each other. Mission planning suggests looking at what will

84 (USMC OFFICER, n.d)
85 (USMC OFFICER, n.d)

be the likely outcome of those engagements, and what is the most advantageous actions of the team during planned and unplanned encounters. How will competitors be engaged, can they be converted to collaborators? Will situations occur that trigger a supporting element to join the main effort or begin some other chain of events? Gathering intel will be a necessity.[86]

- Know thyself by accounting for your own strengths and weaknesses. Focus on your strengths. Ask others for your weakness.
- What support is available for the mission?
- Identifying your own size and strength puts things in perspective. What special skills does your team possess that can be applied to the mission set?
- How can one component support another?
- If there are concurrent missions, how can they be of mutual support to each other?
- The other teams in and around the same environment on their own missions, what is their size and strength? Do they have capabilities this team doesn't have?
- Are there teams that can provide support remotely? What additional skills and talent do they bring to the mission?

---

86 (USMC OFFICER, n.d)

- Are there things special and unique to this circumstance?

In today's economy, collaboration is easier and more necessary than ever. You need battle buddies who succeed when you succeed and are trying to accomplish similar missions.

Supporting elements in the military give the main effort capabilities when they are around. While clearing the valleys of Afghanistan of IEDs, we were happy when we had helicopter attachments equipped with enough hate to stop any firefight we'd encounter. Sometimes the opposite is true: if a key player is out, expertise and capabilities may not be available.

- It's not enough to orient only yourself: the team, it's leaders, and all involved must understand the orientation of the battlefields in which we work.[87]
- Since each leader plans their own mission, informing them early will give them time to prepare.[88]
- In the military, we sandbox everything. Visual aids should be utilized when possible using a basic physical model or a map of the area in question. Just like in the movies, toy cars and figurines help set

---

87 (USMC OFFICER, n.d)
88 (USMC OFFICER, n.d)

the stage to orient the mission for the other leaders involved.[89]

· Keep it simple and brief. The orientation should enable the leaders to understand the context of the environment and how elements will move.[90]

Orienting the leaders puts everyone on the same page. They are able to then begin planning their components of the mission. The most powerful tool to get on the same page is the mission statement.[91]

Mission Statement Paragraph

"The mission statement is a clear and concise statement (one simple sentence) of what the unit is assigned to accomplish."[92]

The orientation to the environment sheds light on potential opportunity or worthwhile pursuit. The vision of the mission must be written out at every level.

The mission statement defines the objective of every team on the mission. It defines the "task and purpose."

---

89 (USMC OFFICER, n.d)
90 (USMC OFFICER, n.d)
91 (USMC OFFICER, n.d)
92 (USMC OFFICER, n.d)

If this cannot be determined, the players cannot know when they are "mission complete."[93]

While developing a mission statement, when, who, what, where, and why must be defined. A time is specified as the point of no return. Diving deeper, we can get a sense of how they fit together.[94]

* * *

"Five Ws"

1. When (time): "The designated time to cross the line of departure."[95] Leaving the wire and exiting the forward operating base (FOB) while locking and loading.
2. Who (unit): involves the team to which the orders will be given, the main or supporting efforts depending on who will receive the order.[96]
3. What (task): the action that the group is required to make. In a changing environment, the task may not always be possible. Imagine your task is to blow up a bridge, but the bridge is already blown up. At

---

93 (USMC OFFICER, n.d)
94 (USMC OFFICER, n.d)
95 (USMC OFFICER, n.d)
96 (USMC OFFICER, n.d)

this point, the team would revert to the purpose for guidance.[97]

4. Where (grid): the environment in which the mission will occur.[98]

5. Why (purpose): "The purpose of the mission statement is always represented by the words: in order to (and can be abbreviated by IOT."[99] The why of the action being conducted is the purpose. Having clarity around the outcome enables the team to react in real time and adjust to changes or challenges in the environment.

The purpose of the mission always carries more weight than the task at hand.[100] Once the task has been completed, the purpose will continue to guide action. The task of each team is to provide an overwhelming amount of support to the main effort. The main effort achieves the key mission objective.

* * *

The main effort's task is the "Bid for success," The go or no-go that determines the outcome of the mission. As

---

97 (USMC OFFICER, n.d)
98 (USMC OFFICER, n.d)
99 (USMC OFFICER, n.d)
100 (USMC OFFICER, n.d)

others achieve their tasks, they will continue to support the main effort until mission completion.[101]

Once the main effort has accomplished its task, the higher level goal or a component of the higher level goal will have been achieved.

On any mission, there is only one main effort. The supreme task and purpose of the universe that pertains to this mission. All others understand that their task and purpose is to support the main effort. Whether or not the team is a main effort or supporting effort is identified and written on the mission statement.[102]

* * *

The mission statement clearly and simply articulates information in one sentence identifying when, where, who is participating, the task and purpose, and if the team is a main effort or supporting effort. How the mission will be achieved is yet to be determined.

---

101 (USMC OFFICER, n.d)
102 (USMC OFFICER, n.d)

Execution Paragraph

"We go through our template of planning of all the things we need to make happen," Donny O'Malley told me on a call talking about the intensity of planning his team goes through to produce a $100,000-picture every few weeks.

"We make lists, spreadsheets, assigning out the delegation of work and putting deadlines to every single tiny little thing." His team plans out how to execute its production, every member taking ownership of their piece in the overall mission.

Subordinate leaders must generate their own plan and timeline to accomplish their effort in the mission. "It's why my stress level is so much lower than it used to be. We've hired the right people, who are amazing, who are really good at this kind of thing and can go through it like a machine," Donny said, describing the efficiency of their process. "They are just like, here's X production, here are the deadlines for the scripts, pre-production, casting...." The team knows what needs to get done.

Like in Donny's example, execution defines the "how to" of achieving the mission. Execution will define the plan overall and sub leaders will develop their own plans to achieve their tasks, decentralizing the planning process and empowering the leaders to think for themselves at every level. Each leader on your team must develop "how" they will achieve the task.

* * *

"This paragraph consists of four subparagraphs: Commander's Intent, Concept of the Operation, Tasks, and Coordinating Instructions."[103] It pulls the pieces together to describe the courses of action and how it will achieve the outcome. You can learn from this methodology of outcomes-based thinking to clarify exactly what you are trying to accomplish and how you'll know when you achieve it.

1. Commander's Intent defines how the mission will be achieved. "This is the part of the order that ties the mission statement and the concept of the operation together (your mission with your plan to accomplish it)."[104]
2. Concept of operations is comprised of the scheme of maneuver and fire support plan.
   * The scheme of maneuver describes how the intentionally "anonymous" pieces and parts begin moving

---

103 (USMC OFFICER, n.d)
104 (USMC OFFICER, n.d)

in the future battle space. It is generic so all involved listen to the entire plan.[105]

- The fire support plan identifies how other supporting elements enhance the scheme of maneuver. Artillery, air support, and EOD are ready to respond at a moment's notice through open communication. Identifying all the pieces and the trigger to start an action, all involved walk away knowing the capabilities and shortcomings of the team.

3. Tasks: "The specific missions to be accomplished by each subordinate element of the unit will be listed in a separate numbered subparagraph."[106] Each specific task becomes the mission for the unit below.

4. Coordinating instructions: "Coordinating instructions are those specific instructions that tie the plan together."[107]

Coordinating instructions are the big picture of how all subordinate units will conduct the plan—how each team will conduct the plan but with no specific teams identified, preventing teams from focusing solely on their part of the plan.

---

105 (USMC OFFICER, n.d)
106 (USMC OFFICER, n.d)
107 (USMC OFFICER, n.d)

Start with the staging area of the mission, describing the series of events that will take place until mission completion. Considerations include how the objective will be approached, in what manner, and by who.

Defining the main and supporting efforts as well as the desired outcome of the mission promotes clarity among those involved in the mission. As the situation changes, the leaders in each element are able to pivot with the purpose in mind.

Administration and Logistics Paragraph

Understand that actions have second and third order effects. When the contact you meet at the convention agrees to have a meeting, where is this taking place, who is control of it, and what other planning must go into effect? The better you understand your battle space and contingencies, the more adaptable you'll be when the time comes to act.

The environment is always changing; identifying potential outcomes in advance and understanding the requirements necessary to achieve the associated tasks enables quick reaction in a dynamic environment. Likely outcomes as well as best and worst case must be well-thought-out. This process occurs parallel to developing value propositions and business models—create many potential eventualities and you'll have more flexibility when the intensity rises.

If there is a medical emergency, who can be called and where can we go? Getting prompt care can be the difference between life and death and is especially important when dangerous activities are involved. Where does the food and water come from for the team on site? What about for others who may be invited to join while on a mission in the field? As supplies are used up, there must be a plan to resupply.

* * *

Each team and individual must have their initial issue of equipment and supplies. As these items are consumed or rendered useless, a resupply must occur to bring the unit back up to one hundred percent.

From refilling water to replacing mission critical equipment, the resupply capabilities must be known and executable. If there are potential issues with the resupply, these issues are reported or addressed.[108]

---

108 (USMC OFFICER, n.d)

Command and Signal

"Specifies the signal instructions for the operation."[109] The signal instructions are the communications plan for the mission. What forms will be used, and what are the triggers creating follow-on actions?

A signal can be any trigger, from a word to a green light flashing. Signals carry deep meaning that can initiate specific actions or inform you if it is a friendly force.

Words or phrases can be used to ask if an individual is in distress, needs assistance, or has everything under control. Anything can be agreed upon as long as the necessary people know in advance and can remember the signals. If possible, it's best to have a format in which individuals can speak privately.

All the members of the team must have a way to communicate and the proper information. Who are the primary points of contact, what are their numbers, and will they be available? When those forms of contact do not work, what are the second and third methods of contact? Equipment always goes down; having a back-up to the back-up helps fight off murphy.

---

109 (USMC OFFICER, n.d)

Ensuring everyone has open communication is important, but protecting information is just as important. Determine what information is internal vs. external, anything that is restricted from being discussed, and proper etiquette when dealing with other parties in the environment to protect sensitive data and promote the correct image.

Well-planned and effective communication fosters teamwork and helps maintain order. It is necessary for success.

In 2019, we have amazing tools like Slack to manage large teams of people. Sometimes, it's not so easy to communicate, and other means must be found.

Coordinating Underwater

Have you ever tried talking underwater? It's a real challenge over any meaningful distance. Instead, while diving, we use hand signals, which makes diving pretty peaceful, since nobody's talking.

We don't all have the same hand signals, either. They change from diver to diver, school to school, and continent to continent. Before every dive we rehearse. We speak with our hands, using the dive signals as we brief our dive.

We make divers with us mimic the signal and say what it means for additional reinforcement. Even the different, interesting types of fish get their own hand signals, which are discussed in the briefing. Over time, they become second nature and another language for those you dive with often.

Each dive is unique and certain circumstances require new signals. If you agree in advance and remember the signal, communication happens.

During our World Record attempt, there were several unique hand signals we developed and briefed before the dive, multiple times. Repetition and practice enable quick response in trying times.

* * *

If the mission is misunderstood by a single person, lives are at risk. "What questions do you have?" is a question we don't hear enough. Giving the entire team the ability to ask questions and clarify misunderstandings.

Team leaders should not simply copy the orders from higher. They must generate their own orders from the provided information, expertise. and research at each level of command.

Summary

The Marine Corps mission planning breaks down into five paragraphs. These tenets are supported by validated assumptions from internal sources and intelligence. Keeping them to a paragraph in length helps to simplify and clarify the process.

Of course, mission planning does not exactly transfer to business. The concepts and ideas of keeping a plan short and empowering other leaders to plan their own missions enable the entire team to understand the mission at hand.

* * *

- "If you actually study it [Marine Corp Planning Process], and embrace it, and make an effort to be great at it, you'll be set up for success for the rest of your life." –Donny O'Malley

- "A leader's reconnaissance is arranged to confirm the unit leader's estimate of the situation."[110] Your assumptions must be confirmed.
- Creating clear, concise missions with tangible outcomes of the main objective enables your team to complete the mission.
- Read the USMC Officers Orders Process.
- Orient yourself to the industry you intend to enter. Identify five potential strategic partners that can enhance your skills. Write a paragraph with relevant information.
- Develop a mission statement paragraph defining the go/no-go purpose.
- Define the course of action of the mission from beginning to end, including the tasks to be achieved.
- Identify the administrative and logistical needs of the mission, including costs or other resources.
- Develop a communication plan with backups if technology or tools malfunction. Discuss and practice signals that trigger follow-on events.

USMC OFFICER. (n.d). *The Operation Order (OPORD) - USMC OFFICER.* [online] Available at: https://www.usmcofficer.com/officer-candidate-school/commission-

---

110 (USMC OFFICER, n.d)

ing-course-seniors/operation-order-opord/ [Accessed 22 Sep. 2019].

Part 3

Mission Support

Every mission requires resources and support. You will rely on your network, human power, the leadership of yourself and others, and finally the culture you build. Like having "air-support" on the battlefield, the topics in the following chapters are a *force-multiplier* to the entrepreneur's efforts.

"If you want to go fast, go alone. If you want to go far, go together," says an African proverb. The people that surround you will be the secret to your success. Customers, vendors, partners, advisors, friends, family, and many others will contribute to the work you do to change the world.

You are needed to make these changes because without you, no change will happen. Building and engaging your network will be the cornerstone to getting started, and you will be the headstone, keeping it together. Asking for help when it's needed, being transparent, and building leaders by being a leader yourself will build the infrastructure to do more.

Part Three scratches the surface of these topics and hopefully entices you to do further research and find out more about how deep this rabbit hole goes.

Chapter 7

Network

Your Social Network

"Taking the sociological perspective, several researchers have exam-

ined social networks effects on venture performance and have found that social networks are important in the creation, growth, and success of new ventures."[111]

Studies indicate the importance of an entrepreneur growing their network. These networks provide knowledge, opportunity, and access to capital. "Often they must rely on social relations to identify opportunities for launching new ventures and to garner crucial information and resources."[112] These networks are important and fortunately they are skills we can learn.

---

111 (Fang et al., 2014)
112 (Fang et al., 2014)

"Political skill reflects personal competency in social interactions and proficiency at applying situationally appropriate behaviour and tactics to influence others, especially in highly uncertain environments."[113]

In the uncertain environment of the start-up, the development of these skills and networks could be the difference between life and death of the company. "During venture creation, entrepreneurs consistently use their social networks to gather information and ideas and to identify market opportunities.[114] To do this, four dimensions were studied;

1. Social Astuteness: the ability to understand social interactions and identify with others.[115]
2. Networking ability: the ability to identify and develop diverse contacts and networks.[116]
3. Interpersonal Influence: the ability to powerfully influence others.[117]
4. Apparent Sincerity: the ability to appear to others as having high integrity and as being authentic, sincere, and genuine.[118]

---

113 (Fang et al., 2014)
114 (Fang et al., 2014)
115 (Fang et al., 2014)
116 (Fang et al., 2014)
117 (Fang et al., 2014)
118 (Fang et al., 2014)

"These four dimensions of political skill enable entrepreneurs to strategically adjust their behaviour to different and changing situational demands, to develop resource-rich networks, to occupy advantageous network positions with access to widely ranging network resources, and to more fully mobilize available resources to achieve desired entrepreneurial performance."[119]

Prioritizing the mastery of these skills in the entrepreneurship environment assists the entrepreneur in broadening, deepening, and diversifying their social networks.

"The three characteristics of social ties that an entrepreneur develops and maintains with various contacts—number, strength, and extent—determine the amount of social capital the entrepreneur can access."[120]

1. Number: "contacts the entrepreneur knows and thinks of contacting when needed."[121]
2. Strength: "captures whether entrepreneurs and their contacts have strong or weak relationships."[122]

---

119 (Fang et al., 2014)
120 (Fang et al., 2014)
121 (Fang et al., 2014)
122 (Fang et al., 2014)

- Strong ties: "involve higher trust, support and emotional closeness."[123]
- Weak ties: "useful for transferring information that is highly scattered or unevenly distributed in the network but typically publicly available."[124]

3. Extent: "reflects the diversity of contacts' backgrounds, including occupation, job rank, education, expertise and professional experience."[125]
- Core: "friends, colleagues, business partners and sometimes family members...tend to have strong ties, long-term, and stable relationships.[126]
- Extended: "weak ties with contacts who have more diverse backgrounds and interests and more distant and fluid relationships."[127]

"Thus, a mix of embedded ties and arm's-length ties provides 'resource-rich networks' with optimal benefits, both increasing access to financial capital and reducing costs relative to networks composed predominantly of arm's length or embedded ties." (Fang et al., 2014) Not all relationships will be strong, which is a benefit. The combination of strong and weak relationships leads to

---

123 (Fang et al., 2014)

124 (Fang et al., 2014)

125 (Fang et al., 2014)

126 (Fang et al., 2014)

127 (Fang et al., 2014)

an optimal result. I've heard it said that isolation leads to death; on the other side of the spectrum, building a strong network leads to success.

Loss of Your Network

Leaving the military, we lose our network. From college, civilians begin developing their skills to develop business networks while the military member is learning to follow orders and to beg, borrow, or steal to get the mission accomplished. This disparity in network-building skills puts added pressure on the veteran entrepreneur to develop a new set of skills not learned in their training.

In the study just referenced, the skilled social entrepreneurs "developed a cohesive core network allowing them to rely on their contacts to make key business decisions or important referrals, to provide financial support, and to get tasks accomplished quickly." (Fang et al., 2014) While the military member may have a core network of other military members, the overall diversity of our networks after the military is one-dimensional.

A military member is moving from duty station to duty station, unit to unit, working in various places around the world. Training and warfighting for extended periods of time limit your ability in developing extended networks. We develop close bonds with our fellow soldiers but very few outside of that.

Additionally, it's rare we work with manufacturers, suppliers, customers, or other business-related entities. Not only that, the network you do have is often not relevant after leaving the military unless you are staying in the defense industry.

Without a network in place, the road to a successful start-up will be much more challenging. You must begin developing your civilian network, being sure to include all the stakeholders identified in your business model.

Education and Networking

"I thought I'd go to grad school because I didn't have any other previous business experience," Stephen Calk, former US Army helicopter pilot and CEO of Federal Savings Bank of Chicago told me in an interview. "I was lucky enough to apply and be accepted into Northwestern Graduate School of Business," Stephen described his transition from the military into business and business school.

"My father, being somewhat of a self-starter, he always told me, 'If you're gonna go into business, go into business for yourself.'" Stephen recalled the wisdom of his father. "No matter how successful you are, at the end of the day, there are a lot of people getting paid before you." Knowing he wanted to start his own business, he had a lot to learn.

Going to school would provide not only education, but also feedback from his peers. "If I'm going to start this business, when I start grad school, I'm going to have seventy consultants to bounce ideas off of....I could run this experiment of being an entrepreneur." If all failed, he would have an MBA and his military experience to fall back on. From the tone in his voice, you could tell he was ready to get started.

I asked him how long he waited to start his business, and Stephen replied, "A couple weeks into grad school, straight out of the military as well." He identified a business that didn't require a lot to get started. "I started a mortgage brokerage business, the barrier to entry was relatively low."

Stephen started his business with $100,000, $35,000 of which came from his partner. Choosing his partner wasn't easy. He needed to find someone with the capital and expertise outside of his own. "So, I was strong in leadership, marketing, sales, and development. He was very strong on the finance and accounting side. I was determined to go to grad school to fill the holes in the Swiss cheese." Stephen described the process of analyzing his weaknesses and finding other people's strengths to fill the gaps. "I continue to do that," he added.

Stephen's dream was to not have others get ripped off like he did in his first-time home purchase. "If I could do nothing more than help first time homebuyers, and make sure they weren't ripped off, make sure they were looked after and make sure they got good advice, maybe they would become thrilled about the brand."

They had immediate success, going on for years. Eventually, he began joining organizations. "As time went on, I had the foresight to join organizations like The Young Presidents Organization." Stephen referenced and organization who describes itself as "the premier global leadership organization for more than 28,000 chief executives in over 130 countries and the global platform for them to engage, learn, and grow."[128]

---

128 (YPO, 2019)

When Stephen became qualified to join, he thought he was too busy and didn't realize other CEO peers were, as he says it, "instrumental to be learning from other leaders and other entrepreneurs." The individuals in his personal network, didn't have the correct expertise.

"I got some good information, there was nothing like dealing with peers who had personnel issues, payroll issues, financing issues, growth issues, and tech issues." Stephen's ability to learn from his peers assists him in his quest of being a lifelong learner.

"Many years later I was accepted into Harvard Business School." Stephen was accepted into a nine-year program to expand his knowledge and his network. "That allowed me to develop not only a national, but an international network." Stephen gives a lot of credit to this education and the network it provided. "It was at on of those sessions, near in the last couple of years before I graduated, where I found out about the Dodd Frank Financial Reform Act, and the impact that was going to have on our industry," Stephen said. It was the knowledge and the network he needed to go on to purchase a bank of his own.

The Veteran Network

Would you ever go on a mission alone? The most powerful part of your network already exists. They are happy to support you, and you haven't even met them yet: the network of veterans that came before you and went through a similar struggle. They know it's not easy, they know the feeling of being lost and alone, and they want to help. The only question is whether you will take the initiative to reach out, be vulnerable, and ask for assistance.

After speaking with several veteran entrepreneurs, I learned they all went through a very similar cycle: change careers, try some stuff alone and fail, build a network, try some stuff with support and succeed.

You can't do it alone—find a few veteran events and groups that seem interesting and start meeting people.

Reach out online through social media or email. Look up veteran-owned companies that are interesting to you. Direct message the CEO on social media or call the company and ask to set up an appointment to discuss how they started their business and any recommendations they would have. Listen.

Make learning from those with more experience a part of your daily habits. Reach out to the community of veterans who achieved before you to expand your network and get much-needed feedback.

The World Needs You

"Some people are confused about my name; I am not one of those Rockefellers," Mark Rockefeller announced from stage at the 2019 Military Influencer Conference (MIC) hosted by Curtez Riggs and his team of veterans and spouses.

The MIC hosts a series of influential leaders and hundreds of attendees in the community who want to give back the lessons they've learned on their journey. Knowing businesses require people, Mark has developed a model to create a movement.

"There are 5Ms for starting a movement," Mark continued as he changed slides. Each of the components have very specific qualities.

1. A **Message** is required and must be soul-touching, challenging, and self-beneficial to share. He cites "Yes We Can" and "Make America Great Again" as examples of these messages. They are vague enough

to apply to everyone and the challenge to achieve the task is great.

2. The **Messenger** must embody the message they are projecting. They must be relatable to the masses but also live in the extreme. They tiptoe the line of what's possible and stand up to a nemesis in the process.

3. **(Wo)Manpower** highlights the need for people. We are the only changemakers. The people must adopt their own version of the message, creating a sense of belonging to the group.

4. The **Machine** maintains the movement with infrastructure, money, media, and tech. Processes are developed to form tactics, techniques, and procedures (TTPs), just like in the military. The machine is continuously replicating.

5. **Momentum** must be developed through exponential growth following a noble self-interest. It must be strong enough to overcome the natural interia of the world.

Mark believes developing these traits in your model will assist you in success and he shares them for good reason. He understands that veterans continue to serve after the military to tackle other problems. Using the 5Ms, Mark believes you can engage your network to create a movement.

"The world needs us to create movements and solve the world's problems." –Mark Rockefeller

Summary

The social network you have may not directly or indirectly benefit your new path into entrepreneurship. Developing, expanding, and engaging your core and extended networks are instrumental to your success.

Intentionally look for others who align with your cause and can provide mutually beneficial relationships. Using political skills, your network can be engaged to support your entrepreneurial efforts.

- Isolation leads to death, on the other side of the spectrum, building a strong network leads to success.
- Skills are involved in building a network: Social Astuteness, Networking Ability, Interpersonal Influence, and Apparent Sincerity.
- Your network is defined by its size, strength, and extent.
- Utilize your time at university to expand your network and get feedback for your business idea.
- Many of the veterans who succeeded before you are happy to assist the next generation, begin your outreach, and ask for help.

- Use the 5Ms to spark the beginning of a movement: Message, Messenger, (Wo)Man Power, Machine, and Momentum
- Read *Brining Political Skill into Social Networks: Findings from a Field Study of Entrepreneurs.*
- Identify three possible mentors that would benefit your network and send them an email or social media message.
- Draw out your current social network, including your core and extended network and include the number and strength.
- Identify which areas are strong and which could use improvement.

Fang, R., Chi, L., Chen, M. and Baron, R. (2014). Bringing Political Skill into Social Networks: Findings from a Field Study of Entrepreneurs. *Journal of Management Studies*, 52(2), pp.175–212.

YPO. (2019). *About YPO : YPO.* [online] Available at: https://www.ypo.org/about-ypo/ [Accessed 22 Sep. 2019].

Chapter 8

Capital

"Just to have an innovative business idea and knowledge in the selected branch of business [is] not enough. In order to implement a business idea, a considerable amount of financial resources is required," said Tomasz Smus in a research paper about financing start-ups.[129]

Businesses need capital for a whole host of items, from payroll to pens, each business requiring its own unique cash flows. At every stage of business, the financing requirements are different.

From research and interviews, a trend becomes apparent. Start-ups typically being self-funded, after some success they obtain additional funding from their friends and family network or by competing in pitch competitions. With continued success and skills in pitching their product, some businesses continue to

---

129 (Smus, 2017)

grow organically while others seek Angel and eventually venture capital (VC) funding. It's not only money they provide.

"Start-up projects and start-up companies are most interesting to those investors who can significantly accelerate the development of the project or product through their investments as well as contribute to strong business relationships which investors tend to have and which are essential for expansion of start-up products," Smus said.[130]

He points out the secondary effects of bringing on an investor. Not only do they now have a vested interest in your success, but they also offer more than just money. Maybe more importantly, they offer their network, their expertise, and guidance while the business grows and develops. An important point to consider is the thought about how this is framed.[131]

Just because an investor is willing to invest their capital doesn't mean that it's the best investor for the start-up. The success of the business will, at least in part, be affected by its ability to raise capital. Research and ask

---

130 (Smus, 2017)
131 (Smus, 2017)

others who have had success raising capital and choose wisely when, how, and why.

Friends, Family, and Followers

Twenty-four thousand dollars was the cost of our beach chair business test in Mexico. At the time, I was just learning about minimum viable products (MVPs) and to me this seemed like it was it. I can assure you, it wasn't!

The manufacturers, shipping company, import company, and personnel are lined up: all we have to do is say go. It is decision time: do we want to do this and are we willing to put our money where our mouth is? Is it a good enough idea that others will invest in it? It is time to put that question to the test.

I start calling my personal network. "There are ten thousand tourists a day at the beach town of Playa del Carmen and not a single place to buy a beach chair," I say, explaining the problem. After discussing the idea and the numbers, most people say, "I don't have any extra money at the moment, good luck." Getting rejected by friends and family can take the biggest blow, but we continue calling. Overall, I only raise six thousand dollars, leaving me to fund the remaining seventeen thousand dollars. I call the team one last time in Mexico. "If you're fully behind me on this, we'll start the project." They are in one hundred percent, so we get started.

Only five months later, we wrap up the project. It is a total failure. Everything went smoothly until the team vanished, leaving us scrambling to get started. After liquidating our stock, we have enough to close the books but not enough to pay back investors. This is the risk they take. If you think rejection is a challenge, go tell your friends and family you lost their money. They will be your biggest supporters and most painful critics and may even support you financially. Start-ups are risky— take that responsibility seriously.

In the beginning, start with the smallest, cheapest test you can imagine. Most tests will fail, and it's beneficial to have the ability to test many.

* * *

"Was that all your money?" I asked Donny O'Malley in our interview. "Yeah," he responded. "Burn the ships, there is no turning back." Thinking about the small risks I've taken in business, I couldn't imagine the stress he must have gone through. "You're a crazy bastard," I responded, blown away by the thought of putting my entire $150,000 nest egg on an idea.

"Truth be told, I'm medically retired, so I could have survived for forever." Donny shed light on the overall risk of the project. Yes, it was his life savings, but he had a separate stream of income to fall back on should he fail. He had possibly anecdotal evidence toward a universal basic income and the risk business owners would be willing to take under those conditions. With $150,000 and a fixed income stream to start, Donny sought out additional funding from friends and family.

"I showed them the plan," Donny continued the story. "They didn't give it all immediately; it was a slow burn." He started a crowdfunding campaign with his own money, and convinced his parents to invest an additional $20,000 in their campaign. He explains that, in a crowdfunding campaign, it's important to show immediate success to gain traction. "Everyone wants to be on a winning team...you don't want the pity donation...you want to be a winner in the eyes of everyone."

"So my parents put in twenty grand within a couple of hours of starting the campaign and that was hug,." he said, describing the next few months. "Then I was like, dad, we gotta make payroll—do you have a couple of bucks? Then he put in some more."

Over time, his parents invested around $150,000 in their project. "My Dad, he's been our controller since the beginning, and so he's looking at the numbers." Donny explains how his father has an active role in the business. Treating the business as an investment, his father made it clear, "I'm not going to give to a losing business, I'm not putting anything into a sinking ship. So, if the ship looks like it's going to continue sailing with my wins, then I'll put it in."

By the end of the campaign, Donny had invested $150,000 of his own money and $150,000 of his parents money and was able to crowd fund $250,000. This funding has enabled him to grow to forty thousand subscribers, and he now self-funds a $100,000 production every six weeks. Raising money from his family and hiring his friends, Donny knows his friends and family networks have been crucial to his business success.

Starting with smaller projects requiring less capital, as they proved their model, they grew with it, and so did the funding needs.

Pitch Competitions

"So in 2014, I was pitching for money, got a little bit in 2015 pitching again...and continued as much as I could until I got to 2017, when I pitched in Atlanta." Leah described her journey of going to several pitch competitions and having success at a few. Leah and her sister owns a female tactical clothing company for military and law enforcement called FEMTAC.

Building her business while working a full-time job has not been easy, especially in a capital intensive business. "The money I've won has been great in terms of building and keeping the lights on...building websites...starting prototyping and sampling." Leah and her sister were building their business when a personal tragedy struck Leah, causing her to take time off the business. Working through her personal struggle, she's once again ready to get out to start pitching to get the business going again.

Pitch competitions are happening all over the world. Not only do they provide an entrepreneur the ability to possibly obtain funding, but also these events are often a good place to network and meet talent and possible future collaborators.

Lending

"There is a problem right now with veterans returning and entering and transitioning to the private sector who want to be entrepreneurs," CEO and co-founder of StreetShares said to me in an interview, reiterating topics he discusses often. "It's very difficult for them to access capital." StreetShares is trying to solve that very problem.[132]

"We set up a platform where new veterans can pitch, in their own words, for a loan," Mark said, describing the process of obtaining loans through their organization. "A combination of investors, some institutional funds, some retail investors—they compete to lend to that veteran."[133]

Due to market and regulatory restrictions, many banks have stopped lending in the less than $100,000 lending range, and this situation is when they step in to provide operating capital. "We provide working capital loans to businesses...that's an ongoing need that businesses have."[134]

While taking on debt can be a dangerous ordeal if done improperly, studies show that access to capital in the form of loans is positively correlated to success.[135]

---

132 (Rockefeller, 2015)
133 (Rockefeller, 2015)
134 (Rockefeller, 2015)
135 (Smus, 2017)

"Majority of the start-up companies try to avoid bank loans as they are usually related to complex procedures and are given based on a company's or individual's credit history and property. Since start-ups are usually founded by young people who most commonly do not own any property, it is difficult for them to obtain a bank loan." Smus points out the misalignment of thought and reality about business lending for new businesses.

Studies show a very high and positive correlation between bank loan and sustainability of the start-up companies.[136]

"Veterans that come back in my generation find it very hard to access capital," Mark said on Hiring America. This challenge can lead them to lending sources that are not always ethical.

When I interviewed Mark, he was passionate about providing access to these loans without the often accompanying predatory nature of some lending institutions that target veterans.

---

136 (Smus, 2017)

"There is a history of lenders taking advantage of veterans with high interest rates," Mark said, disgusted by the idea. Being a veteran himself, this mission is personal to him.[137]

"It's important to recognize that I am a Veteran Entrepreneur as well...I think in five years, we will be the eBay of small business loans."[138]

Angels

Angel investor: An investor in a business venture, especially for one in its early stages. (www.dictionary.com, n.d.)

"It dawned on me—my greatest epiphany moment was, at an early stage of investing, it's not just investing in the company—the company hasn't been around that long." Doug Doan, investor at Hivers and Strivers, an angel investing company, tells me about the lack of information for investing in companies at this stage.

"It doesn't have past performance and it doesn't have detailed financials, and you're just kind of making a blind assessment," Doug continued.

---

137 (Rockefeller, 2015)
138 (Rockefeller, 2015)

Angels clearly have challenges in identifying the next successful start-up and must rely on other approaches. "On the other hand, you can do due diligence on the person," Doug said. Due to the connectedness of the military network, angels are able to peer deeper into the true nature of the individual. "I realized, oh my God, we've got a big advantage; the military world is pretty tight and we can find out about a guy or woman so quickly, because everybody knows somebody who served with them and we can find out very quickly if this is a person with the right stuff."

Say you are the person with the "right stuff." What's the advantage to the business owner of receiving angel funding? Kerr, Lerner, and Schoar conducted a study of two angel investment groups. "Using a variety of econometric techniques, we find consistent evidence that financing by these angel groups is associated with improved likelihood of survival for four or more years, higher levels of employment, and more traffic on these firms' websites."[139]

If survival for an additional four years is at stake, I asked Doug about veterans getting funding. "[If] you're graduating from Stanford, and you had some idea, that

---

139 (Kerr et al 2014)

system out there in Silicon Valley area, the Stanford grads have learned to, you know, invest in their young guys coming behind them because it's a good idea. We in the military don't do that." Doug knows all too well the struggles many veterans face getting funding through raising investment capital through angel sources. "That's what we're changing," Doug said. "These are good investments—we don't feel sorry for them. It's not a grant and it's not a loan—it's not something we do because we're patriotic...we think that investing in these guys and gals, we're going to get a better return."

He gives me a better idea of the types of entrepreneurs he looks for while describing a story about a meeting with Silicon Valley investors who were looking for a "Unicorn" company—one seeking a one billion dollar valuation. Not Doug's team.

"We look for woodpeckers," Doug told them as they erupt laughing. "What do you mean woodpeckers?" they responded as the laughing settles down.

"Woodpeckers are up at three in the morning and start working with a single-minded purpose, banging away at something."

Doug explained to the group of angel investors, "If you saw that woodpecker you'd say, 'That is crazy, that bird is going to blow his head up,' but there is a method and purpose behind a woodpecker and he doesn't ever stop, he is just relentless." Doug continued the analogy. "At the end of the day, this is really hard and we want the guy who's up early, working hard."

Doug puts his money where his mouth is in his belief about veteran entrepreneurs. "I absolutely believe in investment in a vet let company will outperform others." At Hivers and Strivers, they're working to prove just that.

Venture Capital

"The challenges don't go away, they're just different challenges." Taylor Justice discussed his current challenges with growth in our interview. "We just closed our first round of financing, our Series B round, on Tuesday; we're now in this new chapter." Raising capital has added fuel to their already growing company.

"We're going to be at 138 employees by the end of the year—now that we just added another $35 million, we could be 200 people very quickly," Taylor said, explaining that having such rapid growth creates a challenging dilemma. "How do we take this culture that we've built, this product that we built, and now triple it in a matter of months?"

Taylor reflects back on the countless books about entrepreneurship he has read throughout his journey. "This is this place that these people warned us about, of growing too quickly and not building the right infrastructure or not building the right organizational structure." Taylor's team is not looking to grow, just for growth's sake, they want to grow in a meaningful way. "The challenges that we face right now is building in that appropriate way, where we don't lose sight of where we came from."

On his quest to build a billion-dollar business, he knows the challenges in front of him are great and will require another transformation. "The people that invested in us—they think we're a billion-dollar business, and we certainly think we're a billion-dollar business, and so we need to start acting like it. We need to bring on the appropriate board structure and bring on the appropriate talent to get us there." It's clear, Taylor believes, it is the people that will get them there.

Summary

All businesses require capital to operate and that capital can come in various forms, each with their own challenges. Applying the right type of capital to your business at the right time can be the difference between success and failure.

Capital is often raised in chunks over time as your business continues to grow and succeed. The capital you need today will be different than the capital you need when you double in size. Choose wisely and be careful when making these types of decisions, as they are often associated with strings.

- Protect your capital and the capital of others.
- You'll have to invest in yourself early on.
- Your Friends, Family, and Fools provide early support.
- Lending, when used appropriately, improves a small business' chance of success.
- Angels are the bridge between early start-up success and venture capital.
- Business challenges don't go away—they only transform into other challenges.
- Read Tomasz Smus's research: *Sources of SUPPORT and funding innovative start-ups.*
- Use Google Scholar (https://scholar.google.com) to research the most relevant form of funding as related to your business cycle.
- Create a six-slide pitch deck for your business or idea.

- Sign up for a pitch competition in your local area.

Smus, T. (2017). Sources of SUPPORT and funding innovative start-ups. International solutions. *Akademia Finansów i Biznesu Vistula.*

Rockefeller, M. (2015). *Episode 38 - Hiring America featuring Mark Rockefeller, StreetShares.* [online] YouTube. Available at: https://www.youtube.com/watch?v=1uiY-i5ZUvCg [Accessed 22 Sep. 2019].

Smus, T. (2017). Sources of SUPPORT and funding innovative start-ups. International solutions. *Akademia Finansów i Biznesu Vistula.*

Rockefeller, M. (2015). *Episode 38 - Hiring America featuring Mark Rockefeller, StreetShares.* [online] YouTube. Available at: https://www.youtube.com/watch?v=1uiY-i5ZUvCg [Accessed 22 Sep. 2019].

www.dictionary.com. (n.d.). *Definition of business angel | Dictionary.com.* [online] Available at: https://www.dictionary.com/browse/business-angel [Accessed 22 Sep. 2019].

Chapter 9

Leaders

"One of the things I would tell my young Captains, 'As long as you're operating within the scope of my intent within the limits of the law. Whatever mistakes you make, I will underwrite and accept the blame for. If you were outside the law or doing something purposefully to the detriment of someone else, I'll be the Judge, Jury and Executioner.'" –Peter Newell

Decentralized leadership

"An RPG went past eighteen inches in front of my face. I can still see in my mind's eye the burning engine as it goes by," says Peter Newell of Begin Morning Nautical Twilight (BMNT). "My definition of fear has changed." Thinking of his time as a commander in the military, Peter reflects on how it shaped him for the work he does today.

Being the commander in the military comes at a price. "I had nineteen soldiers killed, lost my command sergeant major, lost a company commander and his company XO, all within a forty-eight-hour span." Peter informed me of the losses to his unit while he was in command. Being responsible for so many on the battle space, decisions right or wrong, meant putting his troops in harm's way.

"How do you establish functioning governance and functioning utilities while at the same time fighting off Iranian proxies and ISIS?" All while controlling about 4,500 troops in an area the size of South Carolina. Relying on other leaders, he used his vision to guide the battle space.

"The idea of decentralized control, execution and commander's intent left over from my days...is probably most like what we do today." Peter continued. Like working with elite unites, he must trust his leaders to do the right thing and get the mission accomplished with the tools they have. Peter finds similarity in this and in a start-up.

"As a commander, I can describe the effect I want to see from an operation and define the boundaries of risk I'm willing to take." Defining his intent enables his other leaders to know the outcomes to attempt to produce.

"I can assign resources and define the distribution, at that point really step back and let the leaders manage all of it. To include making day-to-day decisions on how to apply resources to best achieve the vision."

Working with teams across the world, he promotes decentralized leadership and self-governing to operate their team of about fifty. "I think this really does apply to the business world as well, especially when you're spread across a couple of continents." His teams are diverse, and they approach each problem a different way.

Peter leads through other leaders in order to stay agile and strategic while they build and grow BMNT.

Great leaders Inspire Action

"About three and a half years ago I made a discovery." Simon Sinek gave a TED Talk titled *How Great Leaders Inspire Action* in 2010. "As it turns out, there's a pattern. As it turns out, all the great inspiring leaders and organizations in the world...they all think, act and communicate in exactly the same way." Unfortunately for most of us, we get it backwards.[140]

---

140 (Sinek, 2010)

"I call it the golden circle," Simon said as he drew three circles, one inside the other with "what" on the outside, then "how" and "why" in the center. Most organizations and leaders begin their communication from the outside with "what" and work their way in, often never reaching the center "why" they even exist in the first place. In Simon's words, "Very few organizations know why they do what they do." In his eyes, this is a major problem.[141]

"People don't buy what you do; people buy why you do it." He explains that this is why Apple, a computer company, can sell a whole host of other products outside of computers. Back then, it was MP3 players, but it's still relevant today. He explains that Dell and others tried to get into the MP3 market at the time, and, thinking back, he wonders why we would buy and MP3 player from a computer company. "But we do it every day." Simon referred back to Apple. "The goal is not to do business with everybody that needs what you have, the goal is to do business with people who believe what you believe."[142]

He described the brain and the biological systems we've developed through evolution. The neocortex is the newest part of the brain utilized for rational thinking, which aligns with the "what" ring of the golden circle, and the

141 (Sinek, 2010)
142 (Sinek, 2010)

limbic system of the brain is responsible for our feelings and correlating with the "how" and "why."[143]

"When we communicate from the outside in, yes, people can understand vast amounts of complicated information like features and benefits and facts and figures. It just doesn't drive behavior." Simon suggests taking an approach from the outside in to speak directly with the emotional center of the brain and allowing the neocortex to rationalize the decision. This goes beyond customer acquisition.[144]

"If you hire people just because they can do a job, they will work for your money, but if they believe what you believe, they will work for you with blood and sweat and tears." Simon suggests that hiring decision should be made upon the employees belief in the cause.[145]

When these belief structures are in alignment and the leader talks about what they believe in, others will find ways to spread the word of that cause. Simon gives the example of Martin Luther King, Jr.'s famous speech "I

---

143 (Sinek, 2010)
144 (Sinek, 2010)
145 (Sinek, 2010)

Have a Dream," for which 250,000 individuals showed up who had no invitations.[146]

"He went around and told people what he believed. 'I believe, I believe, I believe,' he told people. And people who believed what he believed took his cause, and they made it their own, and they told people. And some of those people created structures to get the word out to even more people."[147]

With a quarter of a million supporters showing up, Simon asked, "How many showed up for him? Zero. They showed up for themselves. It's what they believed."[148]

"Those who lead inspire us," Simon concluded. Aligning the belief structure of employees and customers empowers all involved to follow what they believe, which drives them to action. Go tell people why.[149]

Leaders Building Leaders

"I've got an eighteen-year-old kid, who's, man, he's a rockstar—he just needs to mature a little bit," Casey

---

146 (Sinek, 2010)
147 (Sinek, 2010)
148 (Sinek, 2010)
149 (Sinek, 2010)

Lawrence told me in an interview. He sees the potential in his teammates that they may not even see themselves. "He's a hard worker." He knows, with certain traits, he can mold them with leadership.

"I don't have employees; I have team guys. I have teammates. Employees are everywhere—they're a dime a dozen—but teammates, someone who could potentially be a great leader—they're not just around every corner."

Casey's crew consists of veterans and nonveterans, and he believes this diversity adds benefits to his team. "It really is valuable; the vets indirectly bestow knowledge on the non vets who have been working really hard their whole life and maybe didn't go into the military, but they can teach the vets a couple of things." Casey promotes peer-to-peer learning and leadership.

"My ops manager, he's playing two roles right now. His main thing is to manage the crews, but while he's being developed, he needs to learn to develop his replacement." Casey is enabling his managers to be leaders and grow the business. "So, if he wants to be a full-time operations manager, he needs to develop a team leader that reports to him," Casey said, and he didn't develop the system on his own. He said, "It's like the military." Every level is teaching each other to be better leaders, being mentors for those below them and mentored by those above them.

"That's why I'm in this program." Casey referenced a program he's involved in, teaching business leaders how to grow and scale their businesses. Casey takes his leadership role seriously and, as such, is on a continuous path of self-improvement. "It's like in the military, and you're an NCO and you go to A-Noc or B-Noc," referencing military leadership training at the enlisted level. "Sergeant majors go to Sergeant Major Academy to learn how to be the most successful sergeant major they can be." In the military, each level develops their specific level of leadership.

"They already know how to lead troops; they know how to do their job. Now they just have to fine-tune all the stuff they may not have done in their prior role." Casey signified the importance of building a foundation of knowledge and past experience that is built upon over time. "We're taking what we learned in the military and how to implement that into our everyday business life."

Summary
Leaders allow others to be leaders as well as make mistakes. Giving your subordinates "left and right limits"

enables them to make their own choices while being protected from failure if they stay within the limits. This promotes decentralized leadership and leadership development.

To inspire action in your team, start with "why." The reason your business exists in the first place is the mission you set out to achieve. Starting from this perspective taps into the brain and drives action.

Finally, leadership doesn't stop with inspiring action: you must also develop yourself further while developing other leaders within your organization. Choosing the right people for your team is crucial to survival; developing them as leaders will fuel your growth.

- Give your teams latitude to achieve your vision. Provide resources along with left and right limits.
- Great leaders communicate to their customers by speaking about their "why." They also hire individuals who believe in the mission.
- Leaders must be built into every level of the organization.
- Leaders seek constant improvement in themselves and others.
- Define "why" you're starting a business, and go tell five people.

- Identify one person you can assist and provide mentorship.
- Ask one person to provide you mentorship in something you need assistance with.

Sinek, S. (2010). *How great leaders inspire action | Simon Sinek*. [online] YouTube. Available at: https://www.youtube.com/watch?v=qp0HIF3SfI4 [Accessed 22 Sep. 2019].

Chapter 10

Culture

Small Team Culture

If the military does one thing well, it's culture. From day one, you're getting your head shaved to all look the same; you're forced to wear the same clothes and even walk the same way. Military culture is literally "drilled" into us from the start. After basic training, every unique career field then has their culture built into them through their technical school, and, of course, units have their own culture, too. From memorizing core values to owing "cheer" for "messing up," the culture shapes attitude.

At our EOD unit, or any unit, for that matter, it's important not to make mistakes, as one mistake could be your last. We had a way of dealing with this. For instance, if you were to make a positive statement like, "I can throw a football a hundred yards," whoever hears you say it can challenge you.

If your challenger confronts you and you can't do it, you owe the unit a case of "cheer," cheer being the beverage to your liking. If you can, they owe a case. It doesn't take long for the new brothers and sisters to only make these statements when they know for a fact they can accomplish the feat. We had to ensure the refrigerator always remained stocked with the finest cheer.

"Go arm the bar," my commander tells me the first day at my unit. Arming the bar consisted of following the directions perfectly, which is important anytime you're disarming bombs. Written on a single sheet of paper, the rules are tapped to the wall next to the bell, which when it rang signified the opening of the bar, and the free cheer from our teammates who violated the rules. "How do you arm the bar?" I ask, having never heard of the procedure. "It's on the wall next to the bar—why don't you read them out so everybody is reminded of the rules?" he says with a grin. I look at the wall and start reading them.

"#1 The highest ranking official must approve the bar being open."

Before finishing the first sentence, everyone in my unit crowds around the bar area, bursting out laughing and yelling.

"That's a case!" they all yelled.

Confused and looking back at my commander, he says, "Come on, keep going, we don't have all day. I'm thirsty." I keep reading.

"#2 The pin must be removed from safe and placed on armed before ringing the bell."

I continued through another eruption of laughter and people yelling, "there's another one!" they say as I continue pressing on. "I can't hear you." yells the commander over the cries coming from everyone.

"#3 the bell will be rung once and only once, opening the bar." I continue, practically screaming over everyone at this point.

"#4 These rules must never be read out loud...." I cut myself off, stopping immediately. Realizing what had happened, it was too late—I finished reading the rest of the rules in my head but, by the end of my first day, I owed five cases.

Over time, I noticed how effective this nonthreatening solution to solving behavioral challenges was. We all have our habits, some of which are hard to change, creating a fun system of improvement not only helped us solidify things like never forgetting a tool and bonding us together into a unified culture.

Culture Drives Business Value

Culture: "The organization's self-sustaining patterns of behaving, feeling, thinking, and believing."[150]

"Culture matters, enormously," said Booz & Company, now a subsidiary of PricewaterhouseCoopers. "Studies have shown again and again that there may be no more critical source of business success or failure than a company's culture — it trumps strategy and leadership." Although it matters, not everyone is listening. Of the six hundred leaders around the world surveyed, an astonishing nearly fifty percent "reported inadequate strategic alignment and poor cultural support for their innovation strategies," the report continued.[151]

"Our data shows that companies with unsupportive cultures and poor strategic alignment significantly underperform their competitors," said Booz & Company.

---

150 (Wait and Dayman, 2012)
151 (Wait and Dayman, 2012)

Failing to adopt a culture may be the cause of a sluggish business. Getting it right has the opposite effect.[152]

"Companies with both highly aligned cultures and highly aligned innovation strategies have 30 percent higher enterprise value growth and 17 percent higher profit growth than companies with low degrees of alignment," reports the study. The advantage comes from aligning culture with the other aspects of the business.[153]

Quoting a leader at 3M, Booz & Company gave an example. "Palensky articulates his company's innovation strategy clearly: 'We call it 'customer-inspired innovation.'" Connect with the customer, find out their articulated and unarticulated needs, and then determine the capability at 3M that can be developed across the company that could solve the customer's problem in a unique, proprietary and sustainable way."[154]

Identifying what they need to innovate from the customer, they get there through culture. "For over 100 years, 3M has had a culture of interdependence, collaboration, even codependence. Our businesses are all interdependent and collaboratively connected to each

152 (Wait and Dayman, 2012)
153 (Wait and Dayman, 2012)
154 (Wait and Dayman, 2012)

other, across geographies, across businesses, and across industries."[155]

"That's the thing about cultures — they're built up a brick at a time, a point at a time, over decades. You need consistency; you need persistence; and you need gentle, behind-the-scenes encouragement in addition to top-down support. And you can lose it very quickly," reported Palensky in the study, and it's not easy.[156]

Creating Culture—Part 1

"People, more than business plans and physical assets, are really what makes a strong company." –Jay Wilkinson

"In 2002, I was fired from my own company," said Jay Wilkinson, CEO of Firespring, in a TEDx Talk about company culture. He started an internet company in the 1990s, building technology to build cutting edge websites. "We decided we wanted to leverage and ramp up."[157]

Raising one million dollars in capital, they got to work growing. "We expanded to ten cities with people and

155 (Wait and Dayman, 2012)
156 (Wait and Dayman, 2012)
157 (Wilkinson, 2019)

offices." Jay explained their rapid growth and rapid spending of "other people's money." Then, 9/11 happened, and the economy tanked. Jay's business started losing money.[158]

After a period of time, his own board of directors replaced him with a committee. "You can't imagine how it felt," Jay said to me remembering the feeling of rejection. He was determined to get the company back. Masterminding with his family and others, they raised the capital to regain the company.[159]

"It felt really frustrating to me in the early parts and I had to sit down and just beg for forgiveness, be vulnerable and admit mistakes that I had made." Jay tells me in our interview near the end of summer. His investors pushed him to obtain profitability, removing him and attempting to fire another 60% of the company, Jay fought back.

"The first thing we did in this process was open the kimono and share everything with our team. We told them everything we did right, everything we did wrong and we shared our financial statements...we share everything." Jay wanted everyone to feel like they were

---

158 (Wilkinson, 2019)
159 (Wilkinson, 2019)

a member of the team. "We knew the only way to get through this was if we had the mentality that we would all get through this together."[160]

He and his team took pay cuts and salary deferrals where possible. The team pulled together, all protecting each other as one. "If I wouldn't have hit rock bottom in the middle of all that I really sincerely don't know how the culture of organization would have developed in such a positive direction," Jay said.[161]

Jay believes it was his time of failure that bonded the culture he has today. "In the clawing back out of that, and the need to hit rock bottom and climb back out and create an 'it's us vs. the world mentality.'"[162]

He learned that it wasn't the luxury free food and extras like we imagine at all the big tech companies. "Building a company culture is about building a team of people who are committed to the same purpose, the same passion and the same ideals." He argued that the company culture must be "built by deliberate design...or it defaults to who your most vocal employee is."[163]

---

160 (Wilkinson, 2019)
161 (Wilkinson, 2019)
162 (Wilkinson, 2019)
163 (Wilkinson, 2019)

He identifies three steps to developing a company culture:

"Defining your values: Values are meaty and tangible things you can really sink your teeth into." Jay went on to describe the typical values most of us hear about that are bland and uninspiring. Values like ethics, innovation, and teamwork are all important; they just don't inspire employees, and they don't internalize them. He defines the test his values must go through to be accepted.[164]

- Is it distinguished?
- Are you obsessed with it?
- Will it outlive you?
- Can you actually "live" it everyday?
- Are you willing to sacrifice profit to protect it?

"Hire your values": Hiring the wrong person into the company based on their skills is a recipe for disaster. They add a culture screening to their process. "We hire first for culture fit, then for skill fit." For the wrong people that made it through and you missed, "fire them." Jay moved on to the third.[165]

---

164 (Wilkinson, 2019)
165 (Wilkinson, 2019)

"Live our values everyday": His final secret sauce to building culture. Their team has a meeting every day for eleven minutes, during which his teams share the projects they're working on to make sure they're staying on track. "We all know what everybody else is working on, at all times."[166]

After losing his company and buying it back, he created transparency and open communication that would drive his company to growth and his teammates became loyal to the cause.

"Ten percent of our workforce are people who have worked for us in the past have gone on to do other things and come back home." Jay's company, Firespring, was awarded the integrity award by the Better Business Bureau in 2015—he's practicing what he preaches.[167]

"To us, like life, culture is a journey, not a destination." Jay adapted a famous quote about happiness into culture.

Creating Culture—Part 2
"Whether it's a big, Silicon Valley unicorn, a Facebook, Google, Netflix, any company like that, or smaller, more

---

166 (Wilkinson, 2019)
167 (Wilkinson, 2019)

agile regional-based companies that may be not public, they may be private, but yet have an amazing, amazing company culture— every one of them has these down-turns, every single one,." –Jay Wilkinson

* * *

"The fact that sixty-seven percent of people say that they are not engaged at work is a major and massive problem," Jay commented on a Gallup poll about employee engagement.

Jay believes the lack of culture plays a big role in so many Americans' discontent in the workplace. Firespring's culture developed in the worst of times.

In the beginning, "It was accidental," Jay told me in our interview describing the way their culture developed. "What happened early on—we didn't certainly have the structure"; things have changed since then. Jay and his team now follow a framework developed from the eight core questions of *Traction,* by Gino Wickman.

Jay believes these questions are the foundational framework to building culture. His team at Firespring has grown significantly. "We were featured in different publications in Inc., and Forbes, and some of the things is 'one of the best places to work in America.' And the vast majority of those people, by the way, are still with us, even though we're over two hundred employees now."

"A big part of that is, aligning around the eight core questions that every business needs to have in place to feel a sense of belonging and desire to be part of and have an impact." In our interview, Jay rattled off the eight questions in a matter of seconds.

* * *

- "One: your core values—what's your **why**?"
- "Number two is your core focus and refer to that as your **niche**. It's your what—what you do better than anybody else on the planet?"
- "Number three is your marketing strategy—that defines the **who**...are client base? Who are they? What are the demographics and psychographics of these people? How do we know we're reaching the right people?"
- "Number four is what Jim Collins referred to as the **BHAG [Big Harry Audacious Goal]**—it's having that ten-year target out in the future that sets a vision of where we're going and where we want to go as an organization, so that everyone on the team knows what that looks like."

- "Number five is **painting the picture** of what it's going to be like to be part of this in three years—this business, this company—in three years. It's not a list of goals—it's a vision that you paint. If you're going to be here in three years, this is what it's going to look like. It's something people will resonate with and will want to be a part of."

- "Number six is the one-year plan. That's where we get **tactical** with two to seven goals, that as a company or organization we have to accomplish in the next twelve months. These are SMART goals (Specific, Measurable, Attainable, Realistic and Time-bound)."

- "Number seven are the **quarterly rocks**; it's the quarterly rhythm that the company, the business gets into, to make it possible for us to be moving, ever forward on the one-year plan, the three-year picture or the ten-year target."

- "The eighth question revolves around the **issues**. These are the ideas, the opportunities, the challenges, the problems that every business has. And in any company that makes it possible for every single person in that company, to be not only allowed to, but expected to bring those issues to the table on a weekly rhythm where we're constantly talking about them, and identifying and discussing and solving key issues in the business."

Summary

Culture is ingrained in organizations and must be intentionally developed. Creating the right culture will drive value in your business as well as community among your team.

Following the eight core questions gives you a framework to develop culture in your own organization. No matter how big or small, there is always a culture.

- Designing fun positive and negative reinforcement mechanisms into your culture shapes the team.
- Culture adds value to a business.
- You can create culture by following the eight core questions
- Watch Jay Wilkinson's video about company culture: https://www.youtube.com/watch?v=WDFqEGI4QJ4
- Use the eight core questions to develop a strategy for aligning culture in your business.

Wait, S. and Dayman, M. (2012). Company Culture Drives Business Value. *The Value Examiner*, July/Aug.

Wilkinson, J. (2019). *TEDx Lincoln - Jay Wilkinson - Company Culture*. [online] YouTube. Available at: https://www.youtube.com/watch?v=WDFqEGI4QJ4 [Accessed 22 Sep. 2019].

Part 4

Act

Chapter 11

You've Gotta Act

"People seem to be much more interested in collecting ideas, than doing anything with them" –Steve Garguilo

"It's actually really hard to come up with actions for our own ideas. But when it's somebody else's idea, it's really easy to be like, 'You could do this, or this, or this.' The key is setting yourself up so you're getting that feedback from others," Steve continued as he describes action storming, a method of generating actions for other people's ideas.[168]

Sitting at an outside table at a restaurant, they started asking unprepared passersby if they need any problems solved. They received a few generic basic questions they help out with, and then something magical happened. "Can I solve problems with you?" a stranger asked Steve and his small crew of three or four. She joined, and

---

168 (Garguilo, 2017)

they continue solving problems. Pretty soon he realized, there was a line out the door and people are starting to tweet about them.[169]

"Then this woman from Goodwill asks, 'How can we grow our brand?'" Steve immediately replied, "How can you not grow your brand? You have like three hundred stores!" He rattled off ten ideas she could try at various stores. She asked if he could come give a workshop to get more ideas. After giving her ten ideas, she wanted more. She was stuck in ideation, the opposite of what Steve and his crew were doing that day.[170]

"We could have done anything with those Post-it notes, or we could have sat there and done nothing at all, but we exercised our bias towards action to say, hey, let's just try something and see what happens."[171]

Realizing that most people have great intentions after creating an idea but most will never actually achieve it. Some people take the idea and take slow action and others take massive leaps. They dug deeper and identified 3 things about action.[172]

---

169 (Garguilo, 2017)
170 (Garguilo, 2017)
171 (Garguilo, 2017)
172 (Garguilo, 2017)

1. Action is a muscle. Exercise it, the more you do it the easier it gets.
2. Take action right away. We want to set aside time later, and we'll get it done, inshallah.
3. Get feedback. It's easier to generate actions for other people's ideas.

So what is action storming? It's generating action items for other people's ideas. That individual then takes those ideas and goes and implements them. Finding people who will action storm for you is the solution. "Everything in life that's hard, are just a series of steps that are easy. You just have to take that first step." You've gotta act.[173]

You Can Ease In

"If you're looking for a super structured environment, that's not entrepreneurship," Taylor Justice said in an interview. As an entrepreneur, nobody is telling you what can and cannot be done; it must be discovered and done in a way that gives the entrepreneur time to succeed. Staying with a current employer or income stream can do just that.

---

173 (Garguilo, 2017)

"You don't have to quit your job and go start a business to be an entrepreneur. Take care of yourself, pay your bills, take care of your family, and do whatever it takes to make that happen." Taylor takes the counterargument of diving in headfirst and laying it all on the line. Having a stable stream of income enables you to test your ideas without risking your next dinner.

"If you have to do part time for two, three, four, or five years before you have enough to sever that relationship, then don't go in headfirst." In the same way Taylor, Joe, and Paul waited to go full-time until their business could support it, you too can begin testing your business ideas while gainfully employed.

"It's all about figuring it out, but making sure that you're not putting yourself in a bad situation, that you can take care of yourself and your family; everything outside of that, there are no rules, so just make it happen." After making sure you're not devastating your life with a poor financial decision, you've gotta act.

Take That Next Step

Going through the military apparatus is interesting and probably not something one wants to repeat too often. What we do learn, even before arriving at our first unit, is to do one more, and then another, and another, and another. It's truly unimaginable how long it's possible to do pushups and flutter kicks. Thinking back a bit further, I recall the first day of basic training—our hair getting shorn like the sheep we were, standing next to our beds lined up in a row yelling, "YES, SIR" to a man threatening your face with a knife-hand pointed and the brim of his drill instructor cap as black as night and as heavy as steel. "Is it a joke or real?" I often ask myself while proceeding through the mechanism that creates the finest heroes I've had the chance to work with. Who knows—it'll be over soon, and it will be time to be sent off to a new place for some unknown task in just a matter of moments.

The difficulty of your training, ever so slowly increases, driving you harder and harder every day until, at some point, you want to quit. The fear will be too great, the challenge too demanding, your muscles too fatigued. At every level, the military member must either go on or quit. Those are the only options. Finish basic training or quit and get none other than honorable discharge. Carry that rucksack ten miles, or your instructor will make your whole team go twenty. Pass this exam or be reclassified into the worst career field. Learn the training or be left behind without the unit. Watch your step or risk your life. Disarm the bomb or risk an innocent life. It will seem impossible to go on. But you will go on. Your brothers and sisters depend on you.

This is what we demand of our twenty-two-year-olds. How is it possible they continue their mission when all seems lost and the challenge too great? We face these challenges every day. Even now, as I write this book—nine months into the process, it's 10:00 p.m. and I'm working to finish my first draft. Or now, one year into the process, it's 7:24 p.m. and I'm working to finish my final edits. Every combat veteran knows you must embrace the suck and do the thing that's hard. Write the next word, sentence, paragraph, edit the last chapter, get done what needs to be done. Like eating the hard work elephant, one bite of suck at a time.

In the eyes of Jocko Willink, "When there is a challenge... the only way to overcome the challenges that you face, is to start walking. Take that step, everyday, no matter what you are facing. Get up, and start walking. How do you step into bravery? Step! A step towards your fear is a step towards bravery. Don't rationalize anything else. Instead, be aggressive, take action, NOW."[174]

---

174 (Willink, 2017)

Summary

The hardest thing to do is to act. Don't let this stop you. It's easy when your mission is given to you; it's more interesting when you've created your own mission.

Face your fear and act in its direction. Adapt to the environment you find yourself in while staying true to yourself. You know this from the military, from each mission you've endured. Drive on, and, after you have taken the next step, it will be a little easier, and a little easier, and a little easier.

Think about your life up until today—five years ago, it's unlikely you could have achieved what your abilities now afford you. Five years from now, you'll be a completely new human; you will be able to achieve more than you could have ever dreamed—it will be in proportion to the fear you take on between now and then.

The more you gain experience, the more of *The Veteran Advantage* you'll acquire.

- Take an action towards your fear. Step!

Garguilo, S. (2017). *The Science of Taking Action | Steve Garguilo | TEDxCarthage.* [online] YouTube. Available at: https://www.youtube.com/watch?v=hn9so1zVfR0 [Accessed 22 Sep. 2019].

Willink, J. (2017). *How To Face Fear and Step Into Bravery - Jocko Willink*. [online] YouTube. Available at: https://www.youtube.com/watch?v=CgKAFyZNApM [Accessed 22 Sep. 2019].

Acknowledgements

This book would not have been possible without the support of many individuals. I've had the opportunity to interview many entrepreneurs who have shared their wisdom. Each conversation helped me explore what is important to today's entrepreneurs and the veteran community. Here are the individuals who have been kind enough to share their knowledge and expertise:

Donny O'Malley (CEO, VET Tv)

Sam Meek (CEO, SANDBOXX)

Phil Linder (Director of Operations, SANDBOXX)

Steven Calk (Former Chairman and CEO of The Federal Savings Bank)

Jeremie Green (Owner, Island Lyfe Ink Tattoo Studio and Co-Owner, The Gardens Day Club)

Leah Olswizki (Co-Founder, FEMTAC)

Casey Lawrence (Co-Owner, JDog NE Tarrant County)

Mark Rockefeller (Co-Founder and CEO, StreetShares)

Taylor Justice (Co-Founder and President, Unite Us)

Jim Ritterhoff (Co-Founder and Executive Director, Force Blue)

Jonathan Tsui (PNBA Pro Men's Physique World Champion and Former Navy EOD Technician)

William Treseder (SVP of Product, BMNT and Co-Founder of NeuBridges)

Peter Newell (CEO, BMNT)

Matt Butler (Founder, Rollors Game Company)

Jay Wilkinson (CEO, Firespring)

Doug Doan (General Partner, Hivers and Strivers Fund)

Raymond Lott aka The Marine Rapper (Founder, Ninja Punch Music and Recording artist)

I would like to acknowledge Brian Bies (Head of Publishing, New Degree Press) and Eric Koester (Georgetown Professor and Founder of the Creator Institute) for your consistent support and guidance. Stephanie Schneider, Katherine DeMatteo and Ryan Porter for your inputs, ideas and edits. Thank you to those who supported my early campaign financially enabling me to publish: Brandon Wong, Fernando Lopez, Eric Thiel, Ismael Desjarlais, Nick Ondo, Alex Mullen, Dick Larry, Cathy Dahlstrom, Joel Dercole, Laura Harley, Manolo Cabasal, Jordan Cavanaugh, The Floor Guys of Eitzen, Colleen Larkin, Brett Koch, Nneka Okoye, Curt Reiser, Peggy Reiser, Chidinma Okogbue, Craig Chavis, Katherine Edershein, Carrie Gillen, Miki Kurimoto, Rhett Knight, Rohin Shahi, Leah Olszewski, Diane Wolfe, Crystal Bechtel, Neil Fiest, Eddie Gebre, Matt Butler, Justin Blake, Taylor Justice, Peter Newell, William Treseder, Richard Killough, Jeanette Hoeg, Josh Nason, John Balkam, Eric Koester, Erin Jernigan, Phil Kramer, Wendell Wright and Brian Bezalel. Finally, I would like to thank my Mom and Dad for supporting me through every journey in life.

Appendix

Introduction:

The Veterans Metrics Initiative. (2018, June 6). The Henry M. Jackson Foundation for the Advancement of Military Medicine. Retrieved from http://www.hjfcp3.org/site/ assets/files/1485/ tvmi_fact_sheet.pdf

Department of Veterans Affairs (2015). *Table 7L: VETPOP2016 LIVING VETERANS BY STATE, PERIOD OF SERVICE, GENDER, 2015–2045.*

Castro, C. A., Kintzle, S., & Hassan, A. (2014). The State of

the American Veteran: The Los Angeles County Veterans

Study. Retrieved from http://cir.usc.edu/wp-content/

uploads/2013/10/USC010_CIRLAVetReport_FPpgs.pdf.

Chapter 1:

US Army (2006). *Explosive course for war fighters Training with realism on improvised bombs.* US Army.

26thmeu.marines.mil. (2019). *Cycle.* [online] Available at: https://www.26thmeu.marines.mil/About/Cycle/ [Accessed 22 Sep. 2019].

The Brain. (2008). [film] History Channel.

The RAND Corporation (2013). *Measuring Army Deployments to Iraq and Afghanistan.* [online] The RAND Corporation. Available at: https://www.rand.org/content/dam/rand/pubs/research_reports/RR100/RR145/RAND_RR145.pdf [Accessed 22 Sep. 2019].

Crawford, N. (2018). *Human Cost of the Post-9/11 Wars: Lethality and the Need for Transparency.* [online] Watson.brown.edu. Available at: https://watson.brown.edu/costsofwar/files/cow/imce/papers/2018/Human%20Costs%2C%20Nov%208%202018%20CoW.pdf [Accessed 22 Sep. 2019].

YouTube. (2015). *Irreverent War Stories, Afghan Police Brilliance.* [online] Available at: https://www.youtube.com/watch?v=bPRKWiv3kBo [Accessed 22 Sep. 2019].

Chapter 2:

Carse, J. (2013). *Finite and Infinite Games.* New York: Free Press.

Sinek, S. (2019). *The Infinite Game.* [online] YouTube. Available at: https://www.youtube.com/watch?v=tye525dkfi8 [Accessed 22 Sep. 2019].

Chapter 3:

HBR Emotional Intelligence Series: Purpose, Meaning, and Passion. (2018). *Harvard Business Review Press.*

Reyes, R. (2019). *43INC with Rudy Reyes, Force Blue Co-Founder.* [online] YouTube. Available at: https://www.youtube.com/watch?v=_S4uQ49F5Gc [Accessed 22 Sep. 2019].

Reyes, R. and Ritterhoff, J. (2017). *FORCE BLUE "What More Honorable Thing is There to Do?" -Sgt. Reyes.* [online] YouTube. Available at: https://www.youtube.com/watch?v=h_7bUsmc6iE [Accessed 22 Sep. 2019].

Reyes, R. (2019). *43INC with Rudy Reyes, Force Blue Co-Founder.* [online] YouTube. Available at: https://www.youtube.com/watch?v=_S4uQ49F5Gc [Accessed 22 Sep. 2019].

Silverstone, F. (2018). Finding purpose in life. *Harvard Health Watch.*

Duckworth, A. (2016). Grit: The power of passion and perseverance. New York, NY, US: Scribner/Simon & Schuster.

Guinness World Records. (2014). *Largest underwater human pyramid.* [online] Available at: https://www.guinnessworldrecords.com/world-records/largest-underwater-human-pyramid?fb_comment_id=706040809509847_946125542168038 [Accessed 22 Sep. 2019].

Reyes, R. (2018). *The Lionhearted: Rudy Reyes.* [online] YouTube. Available at: https://www.youtube.com/watch?v=oBDLXL6gEsA&t=1s [Accessed 22 Sep. 2019].

Reyes, R. (2019). *The Real Life Aquaman Rudy Reyes.* [online] YouTube. Available at: https://www.youtube.com/watch?v=C_rv2fSfTJE [Accessed 22 Sep. 2019].

Chapter 4:

Nwaiwu, F. (2018). ANALYSIS OF EMERGING BUSINESS MODELS OF COMPANIES IN THE ERA OF THE DIGITAL ECONOMY. *JOURNAL OF SUSTAINABLE DEVELOPMENT*, 8(20).

Poposka, K., Nanevski, B. and Mihajlovska, E. (2019). THE START-UP PHASE IN SME DEVELOPMENT: MAIN CHALLENGES, MOTIVES AND FINANCING OPPORTUNITIES. *Journal of Sustainable Development.*

Nwaiwu, F. (2018). ANALYSIS OF EMERGING BUSINESS MODELS OF COMPANIES IN THE ERA OF THE DIGITAL ECONOMY. *JOURNAL OF SUSTAINABLE DEVELOPMENT*, 8(20).

Kavadias, S., Ladas, K. and Loch, C. (2016). *The 6 Elements of Truly Transformative Business Models*. [online] Harvard Business Review. Available at: https://hbr.org/2016/10/the-transformative-business-model [Accessed 22 Sep. 2019].

Christensen C. (1997), 'The Innovator's Dilemma: When New Technologies

Cause Great Firms to Fail'. Boston, MA: Harvard Business School Press.

Blank, S. (2019). *Steve Blank: The Principles of Lean*. [online] YouTube. Available at: https://www.youtube.com/watch?v=S4nCY-0H4598&t=14s [Accessed 22 Sep. 2019].

Strategizer (2011). *Business Model Canvas Explained*. [online] YouTube. Available at: https://www.youtube.com/watch?v=QoAOzMTLP5s [Accessed 22 Sep. 2019].

Osterwilder, A. (2012). *A New Approach to Designing Business Models - Alex Osterwalder*. [online] YouTube. Available at: https://www.youtube.com/watch?v=fEnDHgTR3bg&t=551s [Accessed 22 Sep. 2019].

Chapter 5:

Burns, R. and Burch, M. (n.d.). *To a Mouse.* [online] Rcsdk12.org. Available at: https://www.rcsdk12.org/cms/lib/NY01001156/Centricity/Domain/3732/to-a-mouse-translation.pdf [Accessed 22 Sep. 2019].

Leingang, R. (2013). *Marine rapper and photographer reflects on service | News21 Back Home Blog.* [online] Backhome.news21.com. Available at: https://backhome.news21.com/blog/2013/07/marine-rapper-and-photographer-reflects-on-service/index.html [Accessed 22 Sep. 2019].

Hetherington, T. (2011). Into the Korengal. *World Policy Journal,* [online] 28(1), pp.60–72. Available at: https://worldpolicy.org/wp-content/uploads/2010/03/WPJ-SPRING-2011-Portfolio.pdf.

Feynman, R. (n.d.). *Feynman on Scientific Method..* [online] YouTube. Available at: https://www.youtube.com/watch?v=EYPapE-3FRw [Accessed 22 Sep. 2019].

Ries, E. (2010). *Web 2.0 Expo SF 2010: Eric Ries, "The Lean Startup: Innovation Through Experimentation. ...".* [online] YouTube. Available at: https://www.youtube.com/watch?v=i65PaoTlVKg&t=569s [Accessed 22 Sep. 2019].

Pownetwork.org. (1990). *Bio, Atterberry, Edwin L..* [online] Available at: https://www.pownetwork.org/bios/a/a044.htm [Accessed 22 Sep. 2019].

Sutherland, J. (2014). *Scrum: How to do twice as much in half the time | Jeff Sutherland | TEDxAix*. [online] YouTube. Available at: https://www.youtube.com/watch?v=s4thQcgLCqk [Accessed 22 Sep. 2019].

Schwaber, K. and Sutherland, J. (2017). *The Scrum Guide*. [online] Scrum.org. Available at: https://www.scrum.org/resources/scrum-guide?gclid=CjoKCQjwt5zsBRD8ARIsAJfI4Bi4FEil-6US-6cma778tNjTr6BccVzfK1Fl8oyP9nI1aJWxeFHKBGXAaAnYkE-ALw_wcB [Accessed 22 Sep. 2019].

Chapter 6:

USMC OFFICER. (n.d). *The Operation Order (OPORD) - USMC OFFICER*. [online] Available at: https://www.usmcofficer.com/officer-candidate-school/commissioning-course-seniors/operation-order-opord/ [Accessed 22 Sep. 2019].

Chapter 7:

Fang, R., Chi, L., Chen, M. and Baron, R. (2014). Bringing Political Skill into Social Networks: Findings from a Field Study of Entrepreneurs. *Journal of Management Studies*, 52(2), pp.175–212.

YPO. (2019). *About YPO : YPO*. [online] Available at: https://www.ypo.org/about-ypo/ [Accessed 22 Sep. 2019].

Chapter 8:

Smus, T. (2017). Sources of SUPPORT and funding innovative start-ups. International solutions. *Akademia Finansów i Biznesu Vistula.*

Rockefeller, M. (2015). *Episode 38 - Hiring America featuring Mark Rockefeller, StreetShares.* [online] YouTube. Available at: https://www.youtube.com/watch?v=1uiYi5ZUvCg [Accessed 22 Sep. 2019].

Smus, T. (2017). Sources of SUPPORT and funding innovative start-ups. International solutions. *Akademia Finansów i Biznesu Vistula.*

Rockefeller, M. (2015). *Episode 38 - Hiring America featuring Mark Rockefeller, StreetShares.* [online] YouTube. Available at: https://www.youtube.com/watch?v=1uiYi5ZUvCg [Accessed 22 Sep. 2019].

www.dictionary.com. (n.d.). *Definition of business angel | Dictionary.com.* [online] Available at: https://www.dictionary.com/browse/business-angel [Accessed 22 Sep. 2019].

Chapter 9:

Sinek, S. (2010). *How great leaders inspire action | Simon Sinek.* [online] YouTube. Available at: https://www.youtube.com/watch?v=qp0HIF3SfI4 [Accessed 22 Sep. 2019].

Chapter 10:

Wait, S. and Dayman, M. (2012). Company Culture Drives Business Value. *The Value Examiner*, July/Aug.

Wilkinson, J. (2019). *TEDx Lincoln - Jay Wilkinson - Company Culture*. [online] YouTube. Available at: https://www.youtube.com/watch?v=WDFqEGI4QJ4 [Accessed 22 Sep. 2019].

Chapter 11:

Garguilo, S. (2017). *The Science of Taking Action | Steve Garguilo | TEDx-Carthage*. [online] YouTube. Available at: https://www.youtube.com/watch?v=hn9so1zVfRo [Accessed 22 Sep. 2019].

Willink, J. (2017). *How To Face Fear and Step Into Bravery - Jocko Willink*. [online] YouTube. Available at: https://www.youtube.com/watch?v=CgKAFyZNApM [Accessed 22 Sep. 2019].

www.ingramcontent.com/pod-product-compliance
Lightning Source LLC
Chambersburg PA
CBHW071521180526

45171CB00002B/339